THE OBSOLETE SELF

By Julian Hamer

© All rights reserved. No part of this publication may be reproduced without the prior permission of the author.
First published, 2015

Dedicated to my beautiful wife Ellen

THE OBSOLETE SELF
Individual Uniqueness and Significance Beyond Egocentrism

By Julian Hamer

Contents

Introduction
1. The Self-Circumscribed Mentality p3
2. The Emergent, Human Ipseity p7
3. The Reorientation of the Human Psyche p13
4. What is Essential is Invisible to the Eye p17
5. Deductive Rationale p23
6. The Original Encounter p27
7. Probity as the Intrinsic, Human Disposition p35
8. Human, Emphatic Existence p39
9. The Tenor of Reality p45
10. Authenticity of the Immanent Presence p49
11. Transformation through Forgiveness p55
12. The Heart as an Organ of Cognition p59
13. Abstract Calculation p63
14. The Urgency of our Time p67
15. The Continuum of Human Existence p71
16. A Volume of Meaningfulness p75
17. The New Human Paradigm p79
18. The Petty Sense-of-Self p83
19. The Necessary Demise of Egocentricity p87
20. Human Sovereign Autonomy p93
21. The Intrinsic Volume p97
22. The Constant Presence p101
23. One Reality p105
24. Corporeal Myopia p109
25. The Twin Restrictions p113
26. Catharsis p117
27. Misperception p121
28. Immanence p125
    By the same author p131

Introduction

Eastern, mystical discipline assumes many appearances but essentially it involves a relentless determination to overcome and break the cycle of repetitive reincarnation through traditional strategy and the cumulative proficiency of self-control. Inevitably, enlightenment is the privilege of a very select minority while the vast, mundane population remains in bondage to māyā and reliant upon the mythology of Divine intervention for solace. The few who pursue the path of sectarian esotericism and renunciation require persistent dedication and single-mindedness.

In Eastern religious tradition the phenomenal world is considered illusory and void of significance. The votary embarks upon a life of esoteric introspection determined to overcome the apparently, chimerical appearance of things through force of will. It is an ideology of escape through an abstemious methodology of every imaginable complexion.

In reality, the material condition of phenomena and human, Earthly existence is not illusory but merely a partial perception. In the West we have come to disregard the intangible dimension of things, preoccupied with the superficial viewpoint. Tangible properties are readily amenable to identification while the qualitative, intrinsic significance of existence and the conceptual origin of organization cannot be assimilated in the same manner. Consequently, incorporeal volume is conveniently dismissed from humanly contrived schemes defining existence because it defies convenient understanding.

Thus, the Eastern proselyte denies the authenticity of appearances while materialistic, Western philosophy advocates the exclusively physical circumstances at the expense of meaning and intrinsic volume.

Through immediate cognition, the human ipseity directly engages circumstances and thereby discovers the overlooked dimension. But the practice of direct engagement requires the recognition of the human, emphatic distinction because it involves a straightforward concurrence between the authentic, human identity and the essential distinction of the phenomenon. Immediate cognition is dependent upon the establishment of the ipseity as our sovereign authority. Similar to Eastern traditional practice and procedure, it requires consistent exercise and application to develop.

However, there is a qualitative approach towards human advancement that is readily and universally accessible regardless of individual status and circumstances. Through openhearted sincerity, we attain immediate and intimate access to supernal beneficence and amity. The full and extensive compass of existence is revealed to us to the degree that we are willing and receptive. Thereby a steady and intimately profound, dispositional reorientation is inaugurated, and we begin to ascertain existence in the fullness of its meaningful pertinence.

1. The Self-Circumscribed Mentality

We determine the essential expanse of existence through the exigency of openhearted sincerity because the susceptible heart eclipses the demeanor of immodest self-absorption that is the critical delusion of the contemporary, human disposition. Furthermore, the unselfish and gracious approach opens the soul to the beneficence of Divine altruism and thereby our obsolete, visceral identification is superseded by magnanimity and goodwill. Thus, we recognize that the authentic condition of circumstances was formerly obscured from our view through a false sense-of-self and instead we begin to harmonize with an antithetical disposition that is appropriate to a meaningful destiny.

Through the immediate and original apprehension of phenomena from the perspective of the human ipseity which is our authentic identity, we discover the intrinsic condition and essential distinction that epitomizes inherent existence. Our viewpoint is established upon our own unique singularity and consequently we recognize the similarly implicit constitution of all other circumstances. Upon this basis we establish direct knowledge of the essential timbre of quintessential reality.

Unlike the propensity of self-interest, the human ipseity is entirely altruistic in the most magnanimous sense of the word because our intrinsic status is without egocentrism. Our singular uniqueness exists emphatically in a condition of existential continuance and cognitive autonomy. Thus, every other thing is naturally distinguished for its similarly essential substance.

Through immediate, experiential cognition, we find

that we possess an intrinsic and singular identity residing in a condition of continuance that is otherwise scarcely discernible because of our preoccupation with an egocentric orientation towards existence. We cannot simultaneously possess two identities, and our egocentrism assumes dominance through familiarity and because of its fundamental establishment as the foundation of the human psyche.

An affected and uncertainly established, spurious identity inevitably detracts from the investiture of our sovereign status. We are unable to identify with our authentic condition of existence because the human, self-absorbed mentality, founded upon existential uncertainty, insists upon its own importance and the assumed necessity of its survival.

Ambiguously and disconnectedly established, the superficial identity would be readily relinquished if we could consistently distinguish and engage our sovereign singularity. But it is tremendously difficult to maintain the realization of human ipseity and to grasp the reality of existential continuance while the false sense-of-self continues to masquerade as our authentic principle and demands constant maintenance.

In order to assuage and supersede shallow egocentrism, we require the establishment of a foundational conviction respecting the certainty of our singular, enduring significance combined with the assurance of a meaningful destiny. The immediate experience through openhearted sincerity of the beneficence and goodwill of The Immanent Presence resolves that contingency. Both our continuance and our substantial prospects are assured because The

Immanent Presence personifies and exemplifies the authentic and future condition of our own existence and we experience those things as inevitably foreordained.

Furthermore, the intimate experience of a profound, supernal amity within the human heart supersedes uncertain self-circumscription. Thereby we find our identity progressively established upon existential confidence to the degree that we avail ourselves of that assurance. The fascination of self-interest is willingly surrendered because we recognize that the illusory, meager sense-of-self does not warrant defense or preservation. Through the immediate apprehension of The Immanent Presence that epitomizes the quality of our authentic distinction, we inaugurate the establishment of the human ipseity as our sovereign identity. A susceptible, sensibility of heart towards The Immanent Presence is sufficient to undermine presumption and initiate a transference and the reorientation of our identity from egocentrism to magnanimity.

The human, authentic, existential status must become reestablished through supernal, imperative influence because we do not possess the prerequisite paradigm to mitigate our egocentric disposition. The discrepancy between self-circumscription and esteem for the intrinsic significance of others is conciliated through the immediate experience and agency of The Immanent Presence. The narrow perspective of self-interest has arisen because we have become absorbed with the sensible, practical aspects of existence at the expense of intrinsic conditions.

Our constricted view is mitigated through Divine

intervention within the human heart. Thereby, we immediately recognize the discrepancy between our egocentric disposition and the magnanimity that arises through existential confidence. Inevitably we commence a deviation of allegiance from self-circumspection towards altruism, and the induction of our intrinsic, autonomous sovereignty is made certain. It is a consummate operation of reformation that merely requires our earnest and willing compliance because essential reorientation from self-preeminence is not achieved through human artifice or aptitude but only through supernal grace.

2. The Emergent, Human Ipseity

The challenge to human emancipation from egotism towards altruism and our destined status of cognitive autonomy and existential sovereignty is intractable self-circumscription because self-interest is essentially uncharitable. We do not inherently and simultaneously possess both the characteristic, human complexion and the necessary altruism and, consequently, we cannot initiate the transformation of our disposition upon our own merits and resourcefulness.

However, there exists a surrogate representation and personification of our destined condition within immanent proximity to the human heart that is approached through our unqualified sincerity.

Ideally, we ought to be able to prove through deduction or at least inference, the existence of an imperative of such vital importance to human advancement. But intangible circumstances are notoriously problematic to qualify because physically elusive evidence is subjectively derived and consequently ambiguous to strict calculation. The manner whereby we approach physically certain situations is not conducive to the exploration of intangible existence.

It is through this conundrum that materialistic, Western philosophy has erred too strongly on the side of caution and all but disregards the intrinsic circumstances of phenomena because they are not physically apparent. Consequently, a perspective towards existence is established that is void of essential significance and meaning because intrinsic value and implicit consequence do not possess physical substantiation and remain incomprehensible to physical scrutiny.

But upon reflection, the impartial observer must concede to the intangible dimension of existence because every physical phenomenon possesses at least qualitative value beyond the obvious material condition and sensible properties. We recognize the elusive proportion through pragmatic experience. If we were to deny the existence of quality because it escapes physical verification then we would find ourselves with an abstractly contrived presupposition that is remote from reality. When we compare an exclusively materialistic perspective towards life with empirically derived, intangible knowledge, we discover a vast discrepancy because, intent upon material exclusivity, we have chosen to emphasize the apparent at the expense of the substantial.

The discovery of incorporeal existence is dependent upon an immediacy of cognition that is without presuppositional bias. We recognize the intangible subtleties of phenomena readily enough when we engage things directly because they reveal the profundity and expanse of the otherwise superficial appearance. It is in pursuit of the recondite that the astute mind discovers both the partisan nature of the materialistic perspective and the neglected dimension that is the authentic and meaningful distinction between phenomena.

Established upon empirical research concerning the disparaged and underestimated significance of the incorporeal, intrinsic magnitude of things, we challenge the myopic perspective of abstractly conceived, materialistic philosophy. The supposition that intangible value occupies negligible significance is dismissed from the moment that we engage existence immediately without presuppositional bias. Through immediate cognition we directly experience the extensive proportion of phenomena and realize that, formerly, we exclusively attended to just one facet of existence while overlooking the full spectrum.

Steadily, we establish a familiarity with the nature of incorporeal existence from our direct exploration of subtle significance. We come to recognize the tenor of authenticity because we become acquainted with its complexion. Thus, when we approach The Immanent Presence through openhearted sincerity, we find that we possess an astute capacity of differentiation between the fabricated and the real because we are accustomed to the distinction. Therefore, it is upon the basis of empiric inquiry that we develop and achieve astute discernment and thereby recognize authenticity when we encounter it.

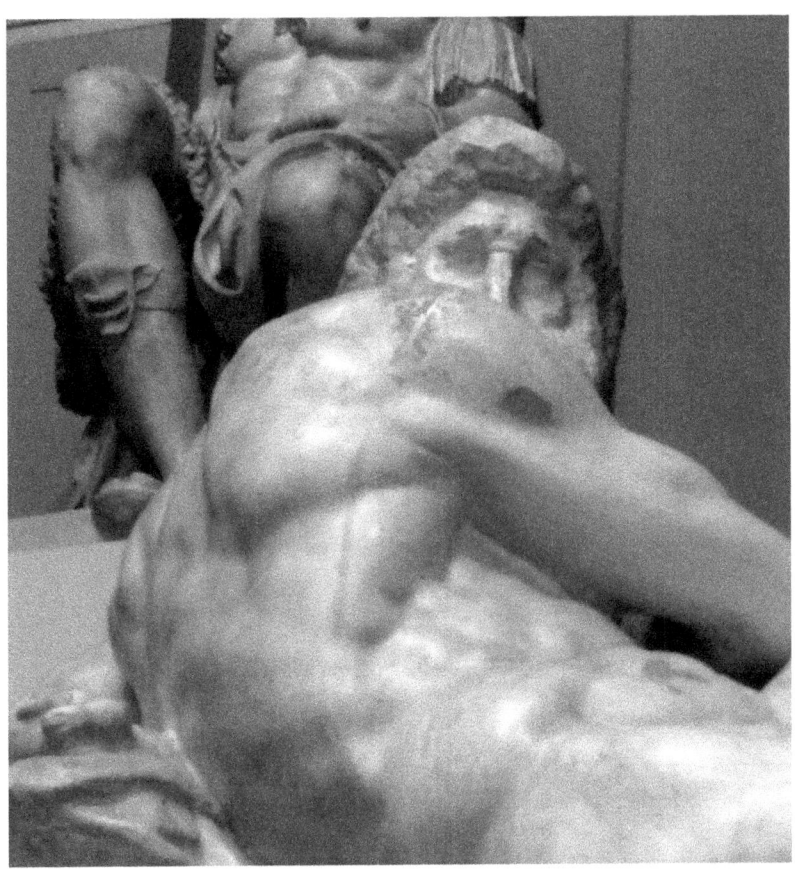

Italian renaissance sculptor Michelangelo (1475 – 1564) epitomized in the sculpture *Il Giorno,* the emergent, human ipseity.

3. The Reorientation of the Human Psyche

We look about us at the human plight and recognize the folly of egocentric motivation. The structures of civilization including art, philosophy and law are steadfastly eroded through the artifices and subterfuge of self-interest. Even religious conviction, founded upon the uncertainties of belief and faith are readily misrepresented and distorted by the passions of sanctioned authority. An entirely contrary position to the essential tenets of a particular, enlightened theology is thereby promoted to accommodate self-interest.

Unless the human soul becomes reestablished upon an entirely contrasting basis to egocentrism, we will find no refuge from adversity and misfortune because the essential deficiency is both visceral and congenital. We shelter beneath the structures of religious conviction and constitutional convention but fail to recognize the temporal and precarious nature of their manufacture, particularly when the principles of rectitude upon which they were established become unfashionable.

The imperative and urgent necessity of our time is the thorough reorientation of the human soul from the conventional disposition and mentality that extols narcissistic, self-interest and celebrates the meager individuality, to the establishment of our authentic distinction. But this is not accomplished through human resourcefulness or artifice. It is the benefaction of Deity alone that transforms the obsolete psyche and thereby charters the establishment of the authentic, human sovereignty. Our task is to make the human heart readily accessible to The Immanent Presence because it is the status of the heart that determines the caliber of our entire nature.

The manner whereby The Immanent Presence ameliorates our obsolete, egocentric disposition and its concomitant ramifications and vicissitudes, involves our amenable participation. It concerns the complete reorientation of the human psyche. Passivity is of meager value because nominal compliance is ineffective in matters concerning the human disposition. Active involvement is imperative because subliminal nature is not swayed by superficial acquiescence but can only be remedied elementally. While we do not transform our essential disposition through our own will and ingenuity, nevertheless we must directly experience The Immanent Presence within the human heart in order to identify and abandon the antithesis and accommodate our renewal.

Correspondence within the human heart between ourselves and The Immanent Presence requires candor and a vulnerability of approach. We recognize when we have attained an immediate concurrence with the Divine through the experience of rapport, and we are impressed by the purgative effect and restoration of our innermost psychology. We cannot simultaneously engage ego-centrism and the disposition of vulnerability because they are contradictory and incommensurate conditions. Consequently, defenselessness towards The Immanent Presence and sincere, openhearted candor is recognized as the essence and substance of human, constitutional transformation.

Communication between the human heart and The Immanent Presence is entirely different from linguistics. It involves complete communication-packages that are qualitatively similar to the concise experience of a successfully articulated artwork. An entirety of correspondence takes place. This is familiar to us because whenever we strive to discover the value of something that is essentially intangible we must apply immediate, experiential cognition that is similarly explicit and precise.

For example, the distinction between two vintages of the same wine or the qualitative acuteness between organic fruit ripened in the sunshine against artificially produced food, is recognized both directly and experientially. We discover that our assessment exceeds an analysis of the merely physical properties. Thus, the commercial substitute may resemble fresh, garden produce to all appearances but qualitatively it remains distinctly inferior. The description of the intrinsic significance of a phenomenon requires the construction of metaphoric and figurative narrative. In the same manner, essential communication within the heart is succinct and eloquent although it does not require terminology.

Thus, if our transaction concerns disquiet concerning another person, we silently engage the situation through susceptible, openhearted sincerity and find that we experience the other from an entirely altruistic viewpoint because we necessarily relinquish self-interest through our defenseless approach towards Deity. Thereby we recognize the situation in its poignant authenticity, and we respond sympathetically. Formerly, our self-circumscribed perspective sustained an illusion of insular and restricted partiality. This misconception is entirely vanquished through openhearted sincerity.

4. What is Essential is Invisible to the Eye

"Goodbye," said the fox. "And now here is my secret, a very simple secret: It is only with the heart that one can see rightly; what is essential is invisible to the eye." The Little Prince - Antoine de Saint Exupéry (1900 - 1944)

Through openhearted sincerity, we enter into an immediate experience of immanent existence. Unlike spatial circumstances, we discover that the intrinsic significance of things resides in a condition of continuance. If we juxtapose the material perspective against the essential composition that we discover through direct engagement, we recognize that our conventional viewpoint is wholly superficial.

The obsolete nature of ego-centrism requires that we profoundly embrace a new disposition of altruism because the former mentality is very much conditional upon an erroneous and narrow view wherein we imagine that the temporal proportion of existence represents the entirety. Positioned and circumscribed within a finite perspective, a moribund and defensive mentality is only further exacerbated.

It is blatantly obvious that the latter view is increasingly pervasive and the source of almost inescapable, pandemic distress.

Two associated approaches merge as we endeavor to effectively ameliorate our outmoded mentality. The first involves the discovery of the human ipseity through immediate, experiential cognition. The recognition of our own unique distinction of existence involves the discernment of our incorporeal and intransient significance which is the enduring portion of our existence that is inevitably denied by an exclusively materialistic perspective. Furthermore, once discovered, we eagerly strive to assert the human ipseity as our sovereign identity.

From the view-point of our authentic and constant status, we recognize the same inherent relevance to be also the intrinsic prominence of others and we attest to their own unique existence. Similarly, we encounter the phenomenal world and discover that all things possess a far greater, essential dimension than that which is revealed merely through their physical appearance.

The second avenue towards an essential reconciliation of the anachronistic, human disposition is through openhearted sincerity towards The Immanent Presence. This is possible because there exists a connate explication within the fabric of existence that ensouls our authentic and destined condition. We render ourselves vulnerable towards The Immanent Presence and thereby our egocentric proclivity is gradually abandoned.

It is here that we discover that through the reorientation of our obsolete, self-centered disposition, our singular and intrinsic distinction becomes increasingly evident to us. But, similarly, we recognize that the necessary, profound transformation of the human psyche is a constant work in progress because it not only involves subconscious reorientation but a qualitative expansion attended by enormous encouragement. The importance of the undertaking is revealed to us as the significance of our authentic identity becomes progressively imperative and compelling.

    We discover the nature, caliber and superior disposition of The Immanent Presence through immediate, experiential attendance. We find the epitome of every virtue exemplified and recognize that we have thereby encountered our own destined condition. We attain this intimate confidence through the re-positioning of our sensibility from the insular condition of egocentrism towards openhearted sincerity and vulnerability towards The Immanent Presence. Thereby the innocent heart becomes our cognitive intermediary and the artery through which our reorientation and dispositional transformation are established. We are reconstructed upon an entirely new premise of magnanimity because through the immediate experience of Divine beneficence, we no longer invest in self-centeredness.

The poignant vulnerability of openhearted innocence and perceptivity is beautifully captured in the painting *Venus and Mars* by the Florentine master Sandro Botticelli (1445 – 1510).

Whether the artist intended it or not, it is through her heart Venus gazes upon the sleeping Mars.

5. Deductive Rationale

The source of human dereliction and insufficiency derives from incorrect self-identification. We assume that our distinctiveness rests upon an insular, self-circumscribed particularity that coincides with our physical condition and spatial circumstances. But our authentic identity is of an entirely different caliber and consequence than that which is implied by our material formation.

There is no meaningful, future prospect for a human disposition of egocentrism because self-centeredness and attendant defensiveness rests upon a merely superficial perception. The erroneous assumption of idiosyncratic and especial merit is a concept that is remote from our authentic, existential status.

We determine the nature of our intrinsic distinction through immediate, experiential cognition. Human ipseity approaches its own essential significance and discovers that merit and status are merely incidental in relation to elemental existence. Singular distinction is recognized as an emphatic, explicit statement that is undeterred by conditions and circumstances because it is integral. Consequently, appraisal and assessment from the perspective of reason is moot in terms of definitive existence.

Ipseity is antipodal to self-centeredness through its explicit, existential status. As a conclusive premise, it exists inherently without need of preservation. Conversely, if human identity is imagined to be of fallible and uncertain value then self-survival remains inevitably imperative and we exist under conditions of profound uneasiness.

We only suppose that our existence is contingent upon our corporeal status because we are assured of materialistic exclusivity. Unable to conclusively reason the existence of the intangible dimension of phenomena, we assume that qualitative volume is merely illusive. We rely heavily upon deduction because we have become convinced of the dependability of rationale and we have learned to deliberate profitably. The suggestion that an experientially direct cognitive approach towards existence might reveal an intangible and immanent magnitude is unsettling because we justifiably do not wish to rely upon guesswork in our approach towards life.

Unfortunately, human reason is only a fallible agency because it is incapable of direct apprehension. Unless we engage phenomena and circumstances originally, we cannot definitively justify the existence of anything. Through scientific discipline and logical procedure we have come to believe that deliberation is a conclusive faculty. We have extended its scope and compass beyond its competence, and we are convinced that we can achieve definitive intelligence concerning existence through methodical deduction alone.

The salient premise of immediate cognition is reorientation from an egocentric perspective towards existence, to the view-point of the human ipseity. The direct, experiential engagement of phenomena and circumstances by our intrinsic, singular distinction is entirely objective because it takes place without any intermediary interpretation whatsoever.

The difficulty lies in the relinquishment of our self-centered predilection and the adoption of an altruistic perspective. This is unachievable through the power of the human will but, nevertheless, it remains within our grasp to foster the transformation of our disposition through extrinsic influence.

The Immanent Presence, as the epitome of the constitution of human destiny, is approached through the heart and not by intellectual effort. While the concept of intrinsic immanence as the substance and amplitude of existence may be reasoned, it cannot be definitively demonstrated as extant because it is not discernible merely through the physical appearance of things. Thus, intangibly extant evidence remains elusive to the readily assimilable affirmation of measurement, calibration and calculation that is most amenable to the function of deductive rationale.

In order to position the human soul within The Immanent Presence, it is necessary to open the heart and through essential, vulnerable receptivity, permit the human, egocentric demeanor to be relinquished in favor our authentic identity. As the ipseity becomes established as the sovereign, elemental significance of our constitution, the intrinsic dimension of existence becomes increasingly evident to us through direct, cognitive experience. But the conversion of our standpoint from self-centeredness to altruism is also a moral one because through vulnerability towards Virtue, we thereby become simultaneously guileless and innocent. We no longer identify with an erroneous, uncertain sense-of-self and, consequently, we find that we have no need to maintain or defend our personification. We recognize existential certitude as intrinsically and infallibly established.

6. The Original Encounter

"Unless we are careful we shall conventualize knowledge. Our literary criticism will supress initiative. Our historical criticism will conventionalize our ideas of the spring of human conduct. Our scientific systems will suppress all understanding of the ways of the universe which fall outside their abstractions. Our modes of testing ability will exclude all the youth whose ways of thought lie outside our conventions of learning. In such ways the universities, with their scheme of orthodoxies, will stifle the progress of the race, unless by some fortunate stirring of humanity they are in time remodeled or be swept away". Science and Philosophy - Alfred North Whitehead (1861 - 1947)

In Nature we observe living phenomena whose appearance is in a constant state of form fluidity. It is vital for a plant or creature to conform to an organizational imperative, irrespective of its metamorphic status of the moment, otherwise it will perish. An organism that is compromised and unable to preserve and sustain the requisite biological structure will fail to continue because impaired, it will be unable to preserve life.

Defective biological organization will necessarily atrophy and perish because disorder renders the arrangement inoperative. The necessity of the full integrity of an organic system is readily observed through empiric apprehension and further qualified by commonsense. The implication of the necessity of a flawlessly disposed, structural and indispensably systemized order, is the existence of an intrinsic complex of essential principles that guarantee the viability of the organism, irrespective of its form appearance at any point in its cyclical development.

The importance of original cognition lies in the capacity to directly distinguish between the peripheral or superficial view and the authentic condition of a phenomenon because we thereby encounter the intangible magnitude.

For example, we enjoy a colorful picture while actually we have, physically before us, merely canvas and color pigment. But we are not interested in the assembly of the equipment but in the substance of the work. The value of the painting is essentially intangible and cannot be found in the paint or the parchment.

It is entirely the same when we consider Nature. The technical researcher scrutinizes the physical conditions of an organism and thereby assumes that the creature is adequately identified solely in those terms. But the intrinsic significance of a phenomenon is not discovered in the construction but resides essentially as the impetus and the particular, qualitative nature of the formation.

The intrinsic value of a work of art lies within the intention of the artist. It is not the physical constitution of the materials but intangible value which the painter endeavors to portray. That content can span through hackneyed, sentimental appeal to a sublime communication of significant merit. In every case, the substance of the painting is not represented by the structure but exists as an alternative volume. It is this elusive, integral component that is the motivation for the appearance and it exists essentially, as the authentic identity of the work.

Similarly, we look at a creature and recognize it by name. We associate the form with that which we imagine we know of the identity of the animal. Interestingly, the layman may prove the more astute in terms of intrinsic identification because of the inclusion of the idiosyncratic character of the creature that is not tangibly apparent. The systematic and analytical approach of zoological scholarship will necessarily be more preoccupied with the physical condition.

We imagine that we recognize what the organism is through associative similarity, drawing upon our memories of myriad comparisons. But we are thereby distracted by what we assume we know and, consequently, we avoid original, cognitive engagement.

Setting aside what we imagine something to be through its affinity with that which we have previously identified, or our accumulated ideas concerning similar phenomena, we approach with a view to discovering its elementally extant condition. Original engagement allows us to discern the particular, qualitative distinction that epitomizes the creature because we discover the distinct impetus that determines its appearance.

The incentive of characteristic, phenomenal form exists imperceptibly as the qualitative manner of its expression. Thus, the intrinsic identity of a plant or creature is found in the idiosyncratic demeanor of its form and correlative, behavioral expression.

In a similar manner to a pictorial representation where the substantial significance of an image does not lie within the blatant physicality of the paper and variously colored ink, we do not find the intrinsic distinction of a creature through a scrutiny of its material properties. The authentic identity is the qualitative distinction and the particular impetus of its expression that is only reechoed in the architecture of its formation.

In Nature, the architecture of form cohesion is the comprehensive synthesis of principles of function that an organism must imperatively assume in order to remain viable. This is the classically recognized archetype which is the organization that determines the successful functionality of a creature and propels it through metamorphic translation while consistently maintaining its viability.

Vastly less consequential but nevertheless parallel, the conceptual law and language of graphic representation, that portrays an otherwise elusive, essential content with paint upon an appropriate surface, may be regarded as the archetypal principles of the art medium of the painter.

Thus, through original encounter, we discover the existence of twin formative incentives that establish both the continuance and the innate, characteristic distinction of an organism. The former is discovered as the operationally efficient, biological systems including the structural organization and integrity that ensures the successful performance of the living creature. The second is the qualitative particularity that is the authentic and inherently characteristic distinction that differentiates one creature from another.

Through the practice of an original, cognitive encounter, we discover not only the status of the existence of phenomena, but we thereby determine the tenor of quintessential reality. Thus, we become increasingly familiar with the authentic circumstances of life which serves as a comparative standard against which all other assertions and attestations of definitive knowledge may be tried by their tenor, for their legitimacy.

Meridian by sculptor Barbara Hepworth 1903-1975
The sculpture enfolds an inner tension that is resolved towards symmetry through the form and gesture of the external structure. This beautiful sculpture serves as an eloquent analogy to the manner whereby organic form follows the characteristic and essential demeanor of the organism.

(Barbara Hepworth: A pictorial autobiography. Tate Gallery)

7. Probity as the Intrinsic, Human Disposition

We engage The Immanent Presence deliberately through openhearted vulnerability, with increasing consistency because we become distasteful and impatient of our moribund disposition of self-circumscription. We recognize the discrepancy between our egocentric condition and supernal unselfishness. Thus, we directly experience authentic morality and find that it is nothing like the self-righteousness and puritanism that arises from human conceit.

A self-centered disposition is not an easy condition to commute particularly if it is misrepresented and disguised as individualism and uniqueness. We presume that our entire significance is insular and exclusive in the manner of our corporeal condition, but the consequence of this conviction is merely a petty counterfeit of our authentic distinction.

The complexion of our intrinsic significance is of an entirely unselfish caliber and remote from the anamorphosis that arises from self-exaggeration. Through openhearted vulnerability towards The Immanent Presence we weaken the artifice and improvisation that masquerades as our uniqueness and recognize that it has arisen merely through an excessive, corporeal identification, to the exclusion of our elemental distinction.

Our own redemptive efforts fail to address the primal malaise of misidentification because our false sense-of-self is not merely idiosyncratic but subjectively inherent. Through varied stratagems we endeavor to assuage our disparate perspective and by training and discipline we strive towards emancipation. But invariably we merely adopt an alternatively disguised presumption of self-aggrandizement. The critical debility remains unimpressed, and we continue to yearn for existential affirmation.

The erroneous but persistent preconception of ourselves as tenuous and uncertainly established, is conclusively resolved through extrinsic assurance at the essential level where the misidentification persists. Thus, we establish an intimate susceptibility towards that which constitutes the substance of our intrinsic status. Through a vulnerable and receptive heart, we hazard our egocentrism to the goodwill and amity of The Immanent Presence whereby we directly discover the quality of selflessness and experience release from apprehension. Thus, we find ourselves liberated from a self-circumscribed mentality that is without prospect or merit and which seeks to justify the significance of a condition that is merely contrived.

The heart is the portal through which the conversion from egocentrism to the immediate experience of our authentic status transpires. The Immanent Presence qualitatively exemplifies our own unique, singular distinction and establishes it nethermost within our constitution as crucial knowledge. Thus, we recognize the false sense-of-self as a vain deception and adopt the compelling assurance of our authentic, existential status in its place. In this manner, we immediately distinguish the full proportion of our own existence and willingly relinquish the counterfeit.

Our self-circumscribed, spurious sense-of-self is only convincing until our legitimate condition is revealed to us and, subsequently, the mediocre value of egocentrism becomes flagrantly obvious. Nothing can impede or hinder our continued exploration, and we yearn to establish its permanence. Upon every occasion when the old, futile sense-of-self intrudes, we turn immediately towards the expedience of The Immanent Presence and through openhearted vulnerability a little more of the former condition is relinquished and superseded by our authentic identity which is our unique, singular distinction. It is this expressive existence that becomes established within the human constitution as our sovereign identification.

If it were correct, as we imagine from the viewpoint of self-circumscription, that humanity is merely egocentrically fashioned, transformation towards altruism would be an impossible undertaking. We would be endeavoring to fabricate something novel with incommensurate components. It is by virtue of our authentic condition that our remediation is assured because nothing complex arises from a merely rudimentary source. It is less our evolution that is at issue but more appropriately a metamorphic reorientation towards our authentic status.

8. Human, Emphatic Existence

Our intention is to describe a cognitive approach whereby we may distinguish for ourselves between the authenticity or falsity of every philosophical and religious interpretation of existence. We do not accept any exposition merely upon the acumen or coherence of a particular conviction because we are well aware of human confusion, duplicity and the mendacity of the egocentric mentality.

For example, the mere affirmation of human, incorporeal continuity is meaningless from a physical perspective because, on the contrary, we plainly recognize our own mortality. The claim of immortality is disturbing because we are unable to determine the credibility of the assertion through conventional perception and deductive reasoning. We must accept the contention on faith, reject it altogether or ignore the issue entirely by cause of its ambiguity.

That which decides us one way or another is not definitive evidence because conclusiveness in terms of intangible merit is unattainable through our conventional and familiar, cognitive faculties. Ultimately our evaluation will merely rest upon accumulated, convincing intelligence for or against our personal conviction.

Similarly, a plausibly argued but abstract philosophy, in spite of exacting illustration and systematic argument, always remains inconclusive because through its conjectural origin, it inevitably persists merely as an unsubstantiated hypothesis. A mathematical equation may be demonstrated as valid through calculation and its value is thereby proven to be true but the distinction between a specious contention and reality is only identified when reality itself is irrefutable determined.

The search for a functional philosophy towards life is certain to be disappointing because the only comprehensive approach is inevitably direct engagement without a philosophical intermediary of interpretation. But an exclusively physical comprehension of existence is insufficient because we are discontented with a merely perfunctory sketch and we quickly discover that the superficial perspective is meaningless.

The volume of something is not found in the shallow perception of its appearance any more than the intrinsic distinction of a human being lies in the physical body. The essential significance of something is imperceptible to cursory evaluation because it resides inherently within the entirety of a phenomenon and not merely within the physical aspect. An extensive scrutiny of the material condition of something will only reveal further minutiae concerning the same narrow perspective. The essential is not found in the most obvious aspects but intrinsically and substantially, as the whole statement of the existence of a phenomenon which includes the intangible value.

Crucial to the direct approach towards existence and the discovery of the intrinsic magnitude that is disguised by blatant appearances, is the recognition of our own essential significance. It is pointless to engage circumstances intellectually in the vain hope of discovering the intrinsic merit of things because rationale is an evaluative faculty and incapable of direct experience. Similarly, emotional evaluation is always subjective and, consequently, brings us no closer to definitive knowledge.

The only manner whereby we can discover the intrinsic significance of things is through the avoidance of both indirect, abstract appraisal and the subjective evaluation of our feeling nature. Thereby we readily engage phenomena without the mediation of the interpretative faculties and the influence of partiality. Unambiguous engagement must occur directly between our essential person and the object of interest. But if we remain stubbornly convinced of corporeal exclusivity and fail to entertain the possibility of a human, elemental and singular distinction that is able to directly encounter circumstances, then we have to rely on the evaluation of circumstances through the very constrained faculties of indirect perception.

If we believe that we are biologically circumscribed without corporeally independent, quintessential significance then we deny ourselves the potential realization of existential and cognitive autonomy because our experiences remain merely between the body and conditions within and external to it. Through the prejudice of materialistic, Western philosophy, definitive knowledge concerning the authentic nature and condition of existence remains impossible.

The assumption of biological circumscription and merely corporeal identity denies us singular distinction. The difference between one body and another is slight, and the global population is enormous. Yet everyone claims idiosyncratic uniqueness; even identical twins. Singular identity is never confused between one person and another merely because two bodies closely resemble each other but everyone owns a separate and particular identity.

The conviction of an exclusively corporeal identification arises from abstract imagination and not through empirical cognition. It is an established assumption that is banished from the moment we cease to intellectually and philosophically evaluate the human condition and engage circumstances emphatically. The entity directly involved and immediately occupied with an event is our own unique distinction. The body is incapable of direct cognition, and objective evaluation is impossible without a straightforward approach. The body is not an entity but it is a vehicle without separate identification beyond the obvious, idiosyncratic variances of a general and common constitution.

Prerequisite to direct, experiential cognition from the viewpoint of the unique and singular distinction of the human being, is the recognition of our original existence and the establishment of our individual particularity as our sovereign identity. Only the human, intrinsic particularity is able to directly engage circumstances because the immediate, cognitive encounter is the sole prerogative of an entity. Faculties do not possess the capacity of pristine coincidence.

We discover our intrinsic distinction through the immediate recognition of our singular uniqueness as an emphatic statement of our being. Upon the recognition of our elemental condition, identification with the transient body becomes severely strained because we discover that our authentic distinction cannot possibly be corporeally circumscribed.

9. The Tenor of Reality

Of itself, human goodwill is an inadequate predisposition towards our further advancement, through its unpredictability and caprice. It is insufficient not because it is without merit but by virtue of its selectivity and constraint. When the human heart opens in vulnerable sincerity towards The Immanent Presence, an entirely more profound perspective is instilled. We are no longer fearful and defensive within the presence of Divine Goodwill because supernal magnanimity is consummate, even concerning our own worst shortcomings.

In much the same manner whereby we immediately engage circumstances through direct cognition, we approach The Immanent Presence without presumption, associative discrimination or evaluation. Through openhearted vulnerability, we directly experience that singular distinction as it really is and not as we suppose. Thus, we avoid characterization and epithet because we do not wish to express our own designation of a phenomenon but desire to discover its particular, intrinsic distinction.

But our research must be conducted upon an empirical basis otherwise we cannot be conclusively certain of the validity of our results. We must establish a standard of reality against which our discoveries may be qualitatively compared.

Through the immediate cognition of biological morphology, we are able to establish a sensibility towards the authentic condition of existence. We recognize the existential status of a Natural occurrence as an ultimately authentic phenomenon because we distinguish the presence of volition that is independent of our own involvement. The living organism moves through a progression of metamorphic appearances in order to achieve a specific end. Thereby we discern the presence of an incorporeal motive, deliberately at work and we recognize a cyclical progression of accomplishment according to very purposeful and consistent principles. It is self-evident that all living creatures must conform to archetypal convention or they inevitably fail and disintegrate.

The identification of incorporeally instigated regulation operating within the vitality of every organism establishes an impression within the observer of something that is intrinsically authentic. Thereby it serves as an unambiguous standard against which the caliber of all philosophical and religious assertions may be essentially compared for their credibility. It is immediately evident when a contention is merely speculative and abstractly construed because we are fully alert to the tenor of that which constitutes reality.

The necessity for the establishment of an independent standard of authenticity rests upon the human tendency to abstractly expound upon existence in a manner that is dissociated from an actual event and, therefore it is essentially fictional. It is to our advantage to hone abstract thought because thereby we are inventive. But if we assess circumstances obliquely and separately from the situations themselves, our explications rapidly become incongruous and obscure. However, with a benchmark established upon an empirically justified autonomous event, we possess the capacity to discriminate between fallacy and certainty.

Furnished with the assured confidence of what constitutes reality we are not deceived by contrived or speculative postulation however sound a conviction may appear and however well it may be argued. We straightforwardly investigate the veracity of a proposition through comparative juxtaposition and recognize when an interpretation fails. If a position is qualitatively incongruous with our own direct experience of essential existence, we recognize it immediately as unfounded.

Thus, through openhearted sincerity we directly experience The Immediate Presence and find that the tenor of our concurrence is entirely of the same quality as that of our discernment of the composite, archetypal principle that ordains biological, metamorphic process. Thereby we discover that the entirely incorporeal, supernal immediacy of Grace is both authentic and absolutely substantial as a vital ubiquity. The Immediate Presence is certainly, physically elusive but the material condition alone is recognized as comparatively superficial. The significant volume and meaning of all phenomena exist intrinsically and distinctly from the cursory, uni-dimensional appearance.

10. The Authenticity of the Immanent Presence

Intangible value and intrinsic significance do not lend themselves well to precise, physical terminology because materialistic terms are inadequate to the task. They apply readily to corporeal conditions because the blatant properties of phenomena are readily amenable to mensuration.

In order to illustrate conditions that are physically elusive yet discernible through immediate cognition, it is necessary to apply the terminology of a particular, artistic medium. By means of figuration and similitude, qualitative value and intrinsic significance may be successfully portrayed, contingent only upon the ability and skill of the artist.

Thus, in order to describe The Immanent Presence, we must first directly and qualitatively experience omnipresence through openhearted sincerity. It is necessary to abandon a physically particular vernacular because it is insufficient. The manner whereby the intrinsic significance of something is portrayed is beyond the capacity and precision of physical analysis, measurement and calculation. The essential is materially inconspicuous and, consequently, it is inappropriate to employ physically concrete terminology.

Similarly, the intellect is ill-equipped to rationalize the existence or nonentity of the intangible dimension of phenomena because qualitative value does not possess physically justifiable evidence. Methodical and deductive appraisal without the substantiation of the facts is little more than speculation. Consequently, the intellect is unable to decisively ascertain the authenticity of phenomena that are elusive to physical substantiation.

We have become accustomed to a perspective towards existence that exclusively condones the palpable properties of things because they are conveniently justifiable and their existence is readily defensible. Thereby we have elevated the superficial at the expense of intrinsic value. Materialistic, Western philosophy has arisen as a counter to the imaginative excesses of mystical and religious inconstancy, typified by superstition and hearsay. Unable to distinguish between delusion and reality, the susceptible are readily at the mercy of chicanery and persuasive misrepresentation.

However, once the intangible significance of things is empirically established as both authentic and meaningful in spite of abstract philosophy to the contrary, the human ipseity is easily discovered by restraining the conventional intellectual and feeling-perceptive, cognitive faculties. That which remains is the unique distinction of which there exists only one. Through immediate cognition, the human ipseity discovers its own singular and emphatic existence.

The reason why it is essential to open the heart towards The Immanent Presence is that the human ethos is improperly established upon a false sense-of-self that is not easily modified. While we relish the experiential recognition of our own incorporeal distinction, our egotism will assume that a glimpse of unique singularity merely enhances its own importance. As long as we remain self-circumscribed, we hinder our further advancement towards authentic, sovereign autonomy.

Thus, we seek to assuage deep-rooted, existential uncertainty through self-aggrandizement because we pursue personal significance where only idiosyncratic characterization resides. We desire respite and nourishment through superficial, physical conditions although the physical appearance, isolated and without essential significance, is void of individual relevance in the light of our authentic status. Only the intrinsic substance of existence affords lasting sustenance because our own authentic condition is not superficial but substantial. Apparent placation offers only fleeting diversion but must be repeated over and over again because it is without the profundity that sustains the human soul.

We become increasingly heedful of the intractable nature of egocentrism and recognize that we are unable to effectively oust it because our false sense-of-self will not permit its own extinction. Therefore, alert to that which constitutes meaningfulness and substance though the immediate recognition of the essential volume of phenomena, we welcome the extrinsic agency of The Immediate Presence that is alone is able to ameliorate our distorted condition.

The activity of direct, cognitive engagement, through the immanent nature in which we find the essential volume of things to exist, also reveals that influence which matures the human soul. The Immanent Presence becomes personally effective within us and ameliorates our petty sense-of-self through openhearted concurrence.

Mindful of the qualitative standard of essential authenticity that we have established from our direct experience of the intangible dynamic of the biological archetype, we open-heartedly engage The Immediate

Presence. We are assured of what differentiates intrinsic reality from abstract intellectual conjecture and feeling-perception and we maintain an alertness to that certain example. We directly determine if our experience of The Immanent Presence is of the same caliber as the immaculate complexity of the Natural archetype. Furthermore, we recognize that the cyclical, metamorphic dynamic that ensures the viability of living creatures is as eloquent as a symphony. Upon the strength of the direct cognition of the independent existence of the biological archetype rests our assurance concerning the authentic status and the meaningful amplitude of existence. We establish a benchmark that connotes a standard of comparison and illustrates the qualitative nature of reality.

It is extraordinary how the long-established conviction of self-circumscribed relevance and the entrenched confidence in an exclusively physical existence, confounds even those who maintain the conviction of an alternative viewpoint. This is because egocentrism and materialistic exclusivity are constantly reinforced while the substantial volume remains strangely elusive from the position of our conventional perspective. Yet, through immediate, experiential cognition we encounter circumstances without the interference of intellectual and feeling-perceptive manipulation. The original cognitive approach offers us direct acquaintance with the actual state of existence.

Every phenomenon possesses intrinsic but intangible significance that is not apparent to the obliquely functioning intellect or through feeling-perception yet it is readily discernible by immediate engagement. Upon the assurance of direct cognition, we can establish a sensibility for the nature of essential reality. Thus, when we engage The Immanent Presence through vulnerable openhearted sincerity, we already possess a sensitivity towards the substantial nature of existence and we are not easily deceived. In the same manner whereby we recognized the contrived nature of abstract philosophy; our empirically assured benchmark of ultimate authenticity provides us with the means to recognize the substantiality of The Immanent Presence without difficulty.

11. Transformation Through Forgiveness

Through the activity of openhearted sincerity within the Immanent Presence, the human psyche is reoriented and transformed by the forgiveness of the transgressions of others towards ourselves. That which we fail to commute in the demeanor of others, festers in our hearts and thereby poisons our potential perspective of magnanimity, with subjective distortion.

Additionally, the accommodation of resentment within the human soul accrues as an aggregate of apprehensive discrimination that hinders the possibility of a pristine viewpoint towards our own authentic status. We fail to recognize the unique distinction of others and, similarly, we are blinded from recognizing our own intrinsic singularity.

The preservation of animosity towards others for their improprieties is indicative of the self-censure by our own conscience because without the shame of culpability for comparative misdeeds and inadequacies, we would not be condemnatory towards others. Our viewpoint is distorted through existential misgiving and, consequently, we defend ourselves fiercely because we fear the further depletion of our already precariously founded self-esteem.

The dynamic whereby we relinquish our own shame is very straightforward. It involves the release of others from our resentment and disdain. However, this is not merely an intellectual or affected exercise, which would be inadequate. But it involves the human, subjective nature and it is within the heart itself that the dynamic must occur.

We cannot self-ameliorate our psyche because that would require that the same preoccupied feeling-perception should reestablish itself on an amended foundation. But the soul does not possess the crucial dual identification that would be required and, consequently, it is unable to administer the necessary curative to its own foundational malaise. The transformation of the human soul occurs through the benefaction of The Immediate Presence that acts as a surrogate of virtue because the necessary benignity required in order to release others and, subsequently, our own perception, is embroiled in antagonism and self-recrimination. Within the condition of our openhearted vulnerability, The Immanent Presence asserts our emancipated and authentic nature on our behalf and effects the transformation of our perspective from self-circumscribed pettiness to supernal love.

Forgiveness of this caliber is the crux of the conversion of the human ethos towards a condition of maturity appropriate to our further development and meaningful destiny. Egotism is established upon a counterfeit identification with a separate significance that does not possess permanent merit because it assumes antecedent value over the singularity of everyone else. From a self-circumscribed perspective, all other people appear less relevant than ourselves. This sentiment is fundamentally established and, consequently, its forced eradication breeds all manner of emotional aberration because the denial of respective significance amounts to an attempted suicide of identity.

The necessary emancipation from self-circumscription must be of a profundity that dispels existential anxiety in order that we may relinquish our false, isolated predisposition and broaden our view to unequivocally encompass the legitimate, human condition. It is achieved through the direct experience within the human heart of The Immediate Presence. The spurious sense of trifling self, binds us through ignorance concerning our intrinsic singularity and maintains an impasse of visceral uneasiness because we recognize the temporal and futile nature of extraneous and incidental existence. Upon our own inauguration, a contrary conviction of overwhelming magnitude is introduced instantly within the susceptible constitution, and sustained as we dismember egocentrism through a readiness to view things open-heartedly.

There is nothing mysterious about this transformation. Indeed, Deity could not transpose us against our will into an alternative, righteous architecture without the destruction of our potential destiny of autonomous sovereignty. Thus, we alter our accustomed condition through the immediate, openhearted engagement of The Immediate Presence and through vulnerability, we welcome our reorientation. Our perspective is crucially reestablished upon an inclusive basis, and we experience the intrinsic and unique distinction of others which overwhelms our former bitterness. Thereby we find that the notion of desiring them harm is lethal to our own disposition and therein we recognize and experience for ourselves the caliber and potency of spiritual love.

12. The Heart as an Organ of Cognition

The difficulty concerning the identification of the transformative dynamic that reorients the human ethos from egocentrism to a magnanimous accordance and sympathetic amity towards others, is its physical elusiveness. We have confidence in that which is physically apparent but we struggle with the concept of complete imperceptibility. The existence of an incorporeal volume that is entirely unapparent from a material perspective is scarcely credible because we recognize that it requires belief and faith in order to be reconciled with our understandable skepticism.

We have already discussed how the open-minded, empirical approach can reveal credible supportive evidence concerning the existence of the significant yet intangible dimension of phenomena. But we are reluctant to entertain the suggestion of an entirely incorporeal existence, that is materially unspecific and completely defies physical inquiry.

However, we are significantly assisted in our researches by the recognition of our own unique and essential distinction. Through the restraint of our conventional perceptive faculties, we directly and experientially discover our singular existence. Subsequently, we find that we are unable to identify our particular identity with the human body or any of its faculties.

Further, we determine from the perspective of the human ipseity, the similarly essential significance of others and the intrinsic dimension of all phenomena. We find that within the physically elusive essence lies the significance of things while the blatant appearance seems to us to be increasingly superficial. Thus, the physicality of an organism belies the unapparent existence which is both its source and significance and the material condition is recognized as the effect and not the origin.

For example, the elemental originality of a native-element-mineral or the singular distinction of color resides more pertinently in the qualitative dimension than in the physical properties. The quality and value of a phenomenon only exists intangibly and, consequently, in order to be definitively identified, it must be discerned through the direct, experiential cognition of the human ipseity which is itself physically imperceptible.

A living organism is possessed of a physically elusive institution that pilots it through a complex of metamorphic progression without obedience to which, the organism would perish. Furthermore, the idiosyncratic distinction of a creature is indiscernible merely from the physical appearance alone but it requires a manner of perception that can distinguish the qualitative entirety of expression of one creature from that of another.

All these things are implied through the physical status, but they are not specifically represented by the solely material condition. They are revealed to open-minded, empirical investigation but they can only be conclusively identified through the immediate cognition of the human ipseity.

However, that which exists entirely without physical representation is far more difficult to substantiate. The manner whereby we discover The Immanent Presence is beyond the capacity of the intellectual faculties to discern and ambiguous to feeling-perception. It would appear that we are without the means to justify the existence of that which is materially unsubstantiated and, therefore, we can but hope that our faith is merited.

The human heart is almost entirely overlooked as an organ of cognition in much the same way as the human ipseity is unfamiliar to conventional perception. Consequently, the heart is imagined to be synonymous with sentiment and the seat of feeling sensitivity. But it is through the direct, experiential cognition of openhearted sincerity that we discover supernal benefaction and our conviction is made certain by intimate concurrence. We are conducted and encouraged away from egocentrism towards a meaningful reorientation. It is in the dynamic of this activity itself that we confirm the authenticity of The Immanent Presence and we realize that if it did not exist we could achieve neither definitive insight nor the corrective ramification of the soul that is beyond our own competence.

13. Abstract Evaluation

Direct cognition is the immediate engagement of a phenomenon from the perspective of the human, individual identification. The ipseity is not the idiosyncratic character or personality but the intrinsic distinction that essentially distinguishes one person from another.

When the intellectual and affective evaluation of a situation is restrained and our accumulated suppositions concerning circumstances are withheld, we are able to engage phenomena elementally and discover their pristine condition. Conventionally, we endeavor to construe and explain our experiences upon the basis of accumulated intelligence and subjective or preferential appraisal. But nothing original is discovered by associative thinking because we thereby already assume a provisional knowledge based upon a lexicon of accumulated information and experience.

Furthermore, we establish assumptions concerning the nature of existence that are abstractly formulated and remotely deliberated from the events themselves. We rationalize and postulate intellectually as if it were possible to discover reality through detached calculation and prediction.

Abstract assessment is an oblique, cognitive approach that assumes that the reflective contemplation of evidence is more effective than empirical practice. But the conclusions of remote assessment are necessarily conditional upon the validity and substance of the contributed information and must proceed in a piecemeal fashion alike to mathematical computation.

The philosophical approach of René Descartes (1596 – 1650) illustrates the absurdity of the abstract consideration of existence and the consequences of the logical, mathematical approach towards circumstances that are not conducive to calculation. Descartes logically deduced that there is no conclusive evidence to substantiate the existence of the phenomenal world but only subjective confirmation. He questioned the reliability of sense-derived information and correctly proposed that everyone perceives things differently because of the variations in the sense organs themselves. But he failed to include human intelligence in the equation. The human mind constantly evaluates and includes discrepancy in its considerations and thereby it is not at the mercy of the inconstant senses.

Astonishingly Descartes had discovered his own unique singularity through immediate experience. But, as a mathematician he was conflicted between abstract methodology that seemed, through rationale, to offer the exactitude of computation and the possibility of intelligence through the direct engagement of human ipseity. Thus, he selected abstract analysis as his primary approach towards existence and failed to resolve the discrepancy between deductive but oblique assessment, and knowledge derived through experientially direct engagement.

The abstract justification of the nature of existence is always inconclusive and ambiguous. Invariably, a hypothetical position will be accepted through the conviction of consensus and not because it is definitively demonstrated as authentic. Compared with immediate engagement from the viewpoint of the human ipseity, abstract conceptualization is akin to measured guesswork.

The reality of a situation is discovered when we approach circumstances immediately from the position of our own intrinsic identification. The first occurrence is inevitably astonishing because formerly we only speculated indirectly about existence but failed to engage phenomena directly. Suddenly, everything appears meaningful and pertinent because we discover its intrinsic significance. The elemental and conceptual volume of things is recognized and we find that value and quality comprise an essential dimension of phenomenal identification.

We consider existence abstractly with predictably, unsatisfactory results and thereby we construct a philosophical perspective towards life that cannot resemble the actuality because it is only indirectly adjudged. Furthermore, founded upon misrepresentation, we approach existence merely to the extent of our conceptual restraints and perceive the world from an accordingly constricted standpoint. From the perspective of the human ipseity, the abstractly contrived interpretation of things appears as anemic and superficial, void of substance because it is only distantly pertinent to reality.

Whether phenomena and circumstances are merely abstractly interpreted or superficially appraised solely on the basis of their physical appearance, is a moot issue in the light of immediate cognition. When the intrinsic person engages phenomena without the intrusion of the interpretative faculties, things are encountered in the actual condition of their existence.

It is unfortunate that the intellect has assumed prominence in areas of elemental existence where it has neither jurisdiction nor competence. But it is inevitable because immediate cognition is a scarcely recognized capability by virtue of its necessary dependence on the viewpoint of the authentic, human identity. Thus, if the subject of immediate cognition is broached with an intellectual whose confidence rests upon deductive reasoning, the narrow mind will endeavor to reduce it to the familiar terms of conventional categorization. Reassured, there the matter will rest upon an assumption of antecedent knowledge without further investigation or interest.

Similarly, the superficial perspective of materialistic, Western philosophy remains confined within determinate limits that cannot afford to permit the inclusion of intangible significance. Thus, the existence of even the most obvious qualitative, human experiences are tacitly marginalized merely because they cannot be physically demonstrated as extant. Should the existence of the incorporeal value of any merit be seriously included, the whole adduced contrivance would have to be reexamined and declared wanting.

Inevitably, the materialist obstructs the way forward towards the vitally significant recognition of the human, unique distinction and through a myopic conviction of the exclusive pertinence of the obvious appearance of things, the essential is entirely maligned. Thus, the meaningful volume and intrinsic consequence of things are conveniently ignored in order to sustain the nonsensical, philosophical illusion of exclusive physicality.

14. The Urgency of our Time

It is quite clear from even a very cursory survey of world affairs, that humanity no longer has the leisure to indifferently dismiss the necessity of a complete reorientation of mentality. The former cultural restraints that offered some measure of social conservation are rapidly eroding as the pursuit of self-interest reaches overwhelming intensity. Indifference replaces consideration while complacency succeeds concern, as humanity pursues personal advantage in the name of individualism.

The heyday of evasion and indolence towards serious introspection has expired and there is no viable future for a humanity that is self-preoccupied because it is an untenable psychology that leads nowhere. Egocentricity is not an option and we have reached a critical moment of moral disintegration as a result of self-indulgence.

The new archetypal dispensation that supersedes egotism is already positioned in such a manner that makes it readily accessible to every sincere and willing heart. This should be of immense delight to humanity because it offers respite from the tiresome vigilance that is essential to the survival of egotism. The tedious nature of the counterfeit human identity is excruciating and barely tolerable as we endeavor to preserve a disposition that is already, long obsolete.

It is plainly absurd to attempt to maintain a constitution that is falsely and deceptively composed and without prospect or expediency. Our authentic distinction and noble destiny of sovereign autonomy is obscured and its realization obstructed by a petty sense-of-self that is without value. There is no obligation whatsoever to cling to egocentrism as if our existence depended upon it because it does not merit the constant, required maintenance and its abandonment is long overdue. To the degree that we relinquish our former self-centered disposition, the new and authentic human status becomes established in its stead. Required of us is openhearted sincerity and vulnerability towards the corrective grace of The Immanent Presence. The conversion itself in entirely in far more capable hands than our own.

It is the disaffected sense of identity with its isolated, self-circumscribed and uncertain continuance that must be made vulnerable to the Immanent Presence in order that it may be superseded by the direct knowledge of the authentic status of our existence. The real human identity is never existentially uncertain because it is an established constant and, consequently, it has no compulsion towards self-aggrandizement because it exists without consternation.

We live under the misapprehension that we endure only impermanently and superfluously in the same manner as the corporeal conditions that we erroneously assume to be the entirety of existence. This induces a fundamental predicament of apprehension that spawns confusion and alarm because we assume ourselves to be provisional and transitory yet intuit otherwise. We are circumscribed by temporal conditions and endeavor to establish our significance and continuance within those parameters. This deception engenders a profound perplexity because we suspect our existential consequence but the physical evidence proclaims our transience. Thus, a conflict ensues wherein we implement all our resources in the defense of an illusory identity that arose through an accumulative oblivion of our immutable status because we identified too thoroughly with our temporary, corporeal condition.

The conviction of human impermanence is not easily dislodged because we have become accustomed to egocentricity as our dominant perspective towards existence. We attempt to reason hopefully concerning immortality and thereby assuage our distrust. But, increasingly, through the persuasion of an entrenched materialistic philosophy augmented by the methodical analysis of the exclusively physical properties of phenomena, we remain unconvinced. The misconception of human, temporal corporeality as our authentic status is further augmented by astonishing technological advances that seem to enforce our resignation to a physically exclusive existence. We close our minds to further contemplation in order to avoid inevitable despair.

The consequences of a myopic, solely material perspective towards existence, is the loss of human signification and meaningfulness. We place our trust in the superficial semblance of things, convinced of their exclusive consequence while we overlook the substantial and essential value. This disingenuous misperception cannot be countered through human ingenuity because, without knowledge of our essential condition, self-circumscription appears as our authentic identity.

Fortunately, the necessary assurance is immediately available through openhearted attentiveness towards The Immanent Presence. Thereby we discover the reality of every contingency and find ourselves steadily reoriented away from the deceptive perspective that has us confined to a trivial existence. We begin to directly and experientially discern the full substance and consequence of existence.

15. The Continuum of Human Existence

The contrast between ceaseless preoccupation with our intellectual or feeling-perceptive deliberation and rumination against the silent straightforwardness of immediate cognition, is striking. Increasingly, we desire the neutrality and tranquility of direct engagement and we gladly restrain the conventional, ambiguous approach. Thereby phenomena are confirmed for their extant condition and not as we merely suppose them to be. The indirect approach becomes estranged and inappropriate because it does not reveal conclusive, essential evidence concerning the intrinsic nature of phenomena.

For example, the conceptual, archetypal origin of Natural organization is denied from the materialistic perspective through philosophical bias. Paradigmatic conformation is not physically evident but merely implied and, consequently, we may freely contest or contend its existence. Our conventional, perceptive approach towards phenomena is consistently ambiguous, and we establish much of our cosmology upon partisan inclination and majority consensus. Thus, a vast volume of existence is concealed from us because we simply do not recognize that we possess the capacity of definitive discernment.

The existential status of the human, unique distinction is a continuum towards which we become increasingly identified through the practice of immediate cognition and, simultaneously, through the aegis of The Immanent Presence within the human heart. We find that within the constancy of our essential permanence we are progressing towards a sovereign autonomy established upon our authentic identity. The ipseity increases conjointly as integrity and probity is established within the human heart and, subsequently, the petty sense-of-self diminishes.

We constantly strive to expedite and facilitate our progress through openhearted concurrence with The Immanent Presence. But if we suppose that our reorientation is instantaneous then we overlook the tenacity of human egocentricity. There is transformation but it is an incremental growth into a new paradigmatic dispensation and not a magical event. Our reorientation is dependent upon our willingness to relinquish our self-circumscribed disposition without necessarily having any idea what the future condition promises which is itself a miraculous contingency. In fact, we cannot possibly know what will occur when we open the heart to reorientation through deliberate vulnerability but we are increasingly encouraged as we notice the progression.

The significance of a human continuum of existence is an incomprehensible concept from the perspective of materialism because it is something that must be immediately ascertained in order to be known. Reason can neither repudiate nor definitively endorse intangible significance, and rationale is unqualified to decide because it is incommensurate to the task.

When something is directly engaged and recognized for its intrinsic condition, we expand our knowledge. But the evaluation of circumstances from the conventional, cognitive viewpoint, inevitably limits understanding and wisdom. Relying merely upon prior acumen we remain restricted within established acquaintance, comparing fresh experiences with our augmented understanding. Through the originality of the encounter, immediate cognition expands our knowledge because it introduces intelligence of which we have no conceptual expectation.

Immediate cognition sets aside established sagacity and does not attempt to reinforce an original engagement through prior comprehension. Things are impartially determined for their elemental singularity, and we thereby broaden our comprehension.

Direct cognition is essential to the discovery of our human, intrinsic distinction and therewith we determine the authentic status of our existence. The expansive nature of immediately derived intelligence synthesizes into wisdom because it involves the original discovery of the constitution of reality. We find reality through the immediate, experiential engagement of our own unique distinction, which is our authentic identity, and the petty sense-of-self pales in comparison. Through the instantaneous encounter of our human, singular existence without the impediment of presuppositional considerations, we enlarge our cognitive approach with original knowledge. Thus, by unique engagement we discover that which was formerly, entirely unknown to us and without precedent. We discover that the condition of our unique singularity is continuous and irrespective of chronology and event, nevertheless, it exists emphatically.

16. A Volume of Meaningfulness

The essential condition of identity of something is not represented physically. The blatant appearance of phenomena is only the superficial countenance while the intrinsic significance remains imperceptible except through immediate, experiential discernment. Cognitive immediacy is established between the human, singular distinction and a phenomenon, and occurs without the intermediary of language. Thus, we glimpse an entire volume of existence that is elusive to exclusively physical evaluation and intellectual interpretation.

Communication concerning the essential dimension of existence is not effectively achieved through physical description because the intrinsic significance of something does not exist in the appearance. For example, the intangible, elemental identity of a native-element-mineral such as iron is a qualitative distinction that is found only indirectly in the tangible condition. The physical properties of something, although cataloged in precise detail, do not include the particular identity because essential meaning resides in a physically elusive condition.

The essential distinction of a particular color remains unexpressed through numerical representation, which is plainly evident when we attempt to describe it in those terms. In order to reveal unique, intangible significance, it is necessary to apply the figurative and metaphoric terminology of the artist. The names bone-white or carbon-black, lemon-yellow or emerald-green divulge the qualitative volume of which we would otherwise remain ignorant through quantification. We immediately know what is meant by bone-white but overlook the unique significance of the color through the exclusive attention of material analysis. Thus, the essential meaning of phenomena is overlooked in favor of the tangible conditions.

The manner whereby the elemental significance and unique distinction of things is revealed, must be suitably appropriate to the nature of intangible existence. We flounder when we try to apply incongruous terminology and reduce essential circumstances to their banal properties because physically precise representation is incongruous with intrinsic meaning. Through materialistic exclusivity, we construct an imaginary cosmology that is sapped of substance because it ignores the intangible proportion of things.

Conducive to the description of the physically unapparent, essential distinction of something, a language is required whose lexicon is composed of emphatic statements concerning existence. In order to supersede materialistic shortsightedness, packages of metaphoric and pictorial depiction are needed that represent the inherent but physically elusive meaning.

Rendered merely in physical terms, the quintessential content of phenomena is disregarded and, subsequently, value and consequence is incorrectly apportioned where only shallow obviousness exists. The very restricted outlook is void of significance and we find ourselves despondent and, imagining that the appearances of things encompass the entirety, we occupy ourselves merely with a pointless shadow of existence that is deprived of relevance.

The materialistic, Western philosophical approach

is an ideology of mechanisms. It assumes a facade of profundity because its approach is considered and measured. Thus, a calculated position concerning the nature of existence is established, and we imagine thereby that we are less superficial than the indifferent person. However, the materially preoccupied mentality remains convinced of the exclusive value of the appearances of things and this absorption has less to do with thought and more specifically with perspective.

Through the scrutiny of the physical constitution of things, we find the apparatus and its workings but thenceforth we mistakenly proceed to evaluate the entirety of existence upon that basis. But mechanics and operational contrivance are inevitably morbid and devoid of essential significance because they concern the procedure and not the elemental distinction. The substance of things is found in the particularity of their whole identity and not through the analysis of their operational and functional properties. The volume and value of things reside intangibly as the particular singularity of their existence.

Through immediate cognition, we confront the characteristic singularity that intrinsically distinguishes one phenomenon from another. We recognize the essential existence of something as a statement that epitomizes the distinctive significance. The existential status of something is unequivocally declared through the qualitative temper and particularity of its expression. It is not portrayed or described in the physical details of its appearance but proclaimed as an entirely complete articulation of its elemental singularity.

The authentic identification of phenomena is only

symbolically reflected in the physical properties. Distinctiveness rests upon the qualitative manner of the particular variation from a universal commonality. But with human beings, identity exists intrinsically as a unique individualism. Through the conventional perception of the material condition, the inherent, existential status of things is overlooked. But when the cognitive perspective is transferred from the corporeally established intellect and feeling-perceptive faculties to the human, singular distinction, we directly encounter the qualitative particularity of things and the singular distinction of other people. Every phenomenal situation is found to possess a volume of meaningfulness that is only implied physically. Through immediate engagement, the entire significance and greater dimension of phenomena are recognized. It does not require explanation or vindication because it is succinctly ascertained as a complete statement of existence.

Analytical investigation of the physical appearance and the properties of things cannot reveal the essential particularity because identification does not reside in the commodity but in the distinction. An artwork is not decided through the materials that comprise its physical condition but through the intangible content that it reveals. This is entirely analogous to the materialistic assumption that the entirety of phenomena is represented by the material condition. In reality, the essential distinction, while physically elusive is, nonetheless, thoroughly extant.

17. The New Human Paradigm

Immediate cognition reveals the authentic condition of the existence of things that is otherwise only uncertainly surmised through reason, feeling-perception or from subjective experience. The results of direct engagement do not require an interpretative intermediary in order to determine what something is because the encounter is original and consequently unambiguous. Unhampered by the usual prerequisite of analytical evaluation, we are able to discover the elemental distinction of things through straightforward coincidence between the human, conclusive singularity and the essential significance of phenomena.

Concurrent with the continued exploration and development of immediate cognition and the concomitant discovery of our own unique singularity remains the urgency of addressing the corruption of human affection. Established uncertainly upon self-centeredness, the petty self assumes an autocratic function within the human constitution that it does not merit and cannot successfully sustain. Consequently, we find ourselves helplessly at the mercy of a misidentification, convinced that our existence is precariously established and ill-equipped to advance beyond self-interest.

In reality, the disparate, inconsonant self that is forced by default to assume governance, is constitutionally incapable of adopting that office because its existence is insecure and its knowledge is merely superficial. Thus, it searches for meaning where none exists and for sustenance that cannot nourish. The self-circumscribed mentality is callow, inept and incapable of further advancement because hollow egocentrism obstructs human progress and must be left behind.

The inadequacies of the self-circumscribed disposition become increasingly evident with the direct, experiential recognition of our human, unique distinction which is of an entirely different caliber and continues without existential ambiguity. But the petty sense-of-self inevitably obstructs its recognition because it is vulnerable and imagines that challenge is mortally threatening. Furthermore, we cannot simultaneously recognize our sovereign, essential distinction and also gratify self-centered affections.

We are humanly powerless to dislodge our counterfeit identity because that would imply destruction to our self-hood, concerning which we are both jealous and defensive. But the time has arrived when we must adopt a capacious, inclusive and worthy identification because, otherwise, we will regress towards degenerate and brutish avarice. Fortunately, the resolution accompanies the extremity.

Our task is to discover The Immanent Presence within the human heart and maintain that open channel in order that the new, human paradigm may become established as our characteristic disposition. Within The Immanent Presence there is no threat to our existence but only kindness and security. Thereby we eagerly relinquish the obsolete, petty self-consciousness that formerly ensnared us because fear for our existential continuity is assuaged through supernal assurance. We abandon the martinet not by self-eradication but through expansion beyond the petty self and attendant reorientation. It no longer matters what happens to our egocentricity because we find ourselves secure and significant without aggrandizement.

Moment by moment we must permit our obsolete, self-circumscribed nature to be superseded by a new designation until it becomes second nature to turn to the Immanent Presence. The metamorphic transformation occurs within the human heart through the installation of a perspective that is without egotism. This status is beyond human capability to achieve because it requires the establishment of an entirely reconstituted psyche that we do not possess. While we do not own the means to achieve reorientation ourselves, its inauguration is entirely of our personal choice.

Through immediate cognition we discover a perspective that is untarnished by the subjective interpretation of intellectual and feeling perception. It is these faculties, compounded by self-circumscription that discolor the authentic composition of existence. Immediate cognition repudiates physically exclusive myopia through the straightforward nature of the direct, experiential approach of the human, unique distinction. But the inhibition of the conventional, critical faculties requires considerable cultivation and the task remains elusive to all but a very few.

However, human passion, affection and self-centeredness are unequivocally mitigated when we submit our psyche to supernal reorientation. Thereby, nothing hinders an unambiguous perspective of existence, and we find things as they exist in reality without human shortsightedness and distortion.

Thus, we rely upon our own determination in order to direct out attention towards the immanency of the exemplary and meaningful viewpoint, but we do not rely upon our own merit and genius. Should we attempt to do so we will have gained nothing of variance with our self-circumscribed condition except a rearrangement of our current, egocentric status.

      Turning our attention towards the Immanent Presence within the heart, we experience the amplitude of existence through direct, unqualified knowledge impressions. This exposure to unalloyed reality instantly alters our perspective from restricted pettiness to altruism. Thereby we expand from self-circumscription to existential confidence. Further, we find solace and nourishment there because essential being requires sustenance of a caliber that is only found quintessentially. Perfunctory superficiality is utterly inadequate and unwholesome to the human ipseity.

18. The Petty Sense-of-Self

From the perspective of existential uncertainty, the petty sense-of-self regards the concept of a human identity deprived of self-interest, in very unsettling terms. It seems an absurd position because it suggests the neglect of personal advantage and self-establishment.

Perhaps there is merit and even justification in that opinion if we imagine ourselves to be solely responsible for our own advancement. There are abounding examples of sanctimony, puritanism and extreme revisionism among those who strive for religious and presumptive preferment yet simultaneously maintain egocentrism. The stark reality is that the human being does not possess the means to self-ameliorate because egotistical reorientation towards altruism is inherently contradictory.

Furthermore, the necessity of a profound, dispositional transformation is avoided if we assume that we possess an option. The inadequacy of the human, self-circumscribed orientation is obvious upon even the most cursory examination of human affairs. Human renewal is less a matter of preference but more one of acute urgency. Our present trajectory bodes ominously for our advancement because self-interest increasingly assumes precedence over conscience, convention and scruple. The inevitable consequence of the exclusive pursuit of self-advantage without the audit of principle and consideration is clearly fractious and foreshadows the disintegration of civil cohesion.

However, self-abnegation inevitably produces a mere distortion of the same egocentricity from which we recoil. It is obviously counter-productive if the human psyche endeavors to transform itself because it does not address the matter of essential misidentification. The petty sense-of-self does not need to be eradicated of its self-preoccupation but expanded to such a degree that it is no longer anxious for its survival nor cares for personal preference.

    This extraordinary magnanimity does not originate with human resolution but coincides with the direct experience of supernal goodwill within the accessible human heart. If the origin of selflessness were merely human, it would be inevitably disfigured because that which is essential to the individual transformation is imperceptible within a constitution that is preoccupied with its own expediency.

    The necessity of the profound, constitutional reorientation of the human psyche is obvious. The difficulty lies in the proposition that the modification of the soul away from self-circumscription towards altruism, is performed by an external entity. Furthermore, that entity supposedly exists in an immanent condition to the mortal, human being.

    In point of fact, the immanency that we are describing is inaccessible to conventional rationale and cannot be decisively identified through reason because it is found only through the accessible, human heart. Thus, it is the earnest recognition that the barrier to our further advancement lies within our own obsolete ethos that inaugurates reorientation. The intellect may contend differently upon the reexamination of evidence and upon an alternative divergence of information, but it can never definitively demonstrate the existence of Divine aegis one way or another because its confirmation or dismissal lies beyond the scope of argumentation.

It is fortunate that the substantiation of the authenticity of the essential, transformative dynamic rests with every individual and is confirmed within the innermost basis of the human soul. The tendency towards misrepresentation, elaboration and duplicity is a notorious human tendency even when no conceit is intended. On the one hand, materialistic, Western philosophical bias derides everything that advocates intangible reality while other sectarian, doctrinal champions manage to distort and obscure the simplicity of the approach. The metamorphosis of the human disposition from self-circumscription towards altruism becomes something inane and vague, superimposed by imaginative fiction.

In matters that are vastly consequential to the individual, it behooves us to authenticate their consequence for ourselves. The approach is immensely practical, but we must be certain to investigate it profoundly and wholeheartedly because nothing comes of flippancy.

Our inquiries commence within the far reaches of a receptive heart where we utter sincerity holds sway and wherein the dynamic of soul-transformation is necessarily inaugurated. Consequently, unless we earnestly and wholeheartedly approach the situation ourselves we cannot possibly presume any practical knowledge on the subject, and through ignorance, we remain unfitted to adjudicate and resolve the merit of the issue.

19. The Necessary Demise of Egocentricity

Through deliberate susceptibility, the open heart is established as the uncontaminated locus of our identification wherein we coincide with the corrective of supernal reorientation. We position ourselves within the milieu that will take us forward from egocentricity to an expansive perspective towards existence, that is our intended condition. Thereby we readily abandon self-circumscription because we recognize the precarious premise of the mentality of personal exclusivity, as entirely counter to reality.

A misperception has become established within the human ethos through our exaggerated identification with human corporeality and pervasive materialism, that presents an impasse without the possibility of reparation because our prevailing faculties are insufficient to the task. We imagine we can reason our way out of egocentric subjugation and if the argument appears to hold, we will somehow manage our own emancipation. But this is misguided. The intellectual comprehension of an alternative position does not effect the necessary transformation but merely offers an understanding of a potential dynamic yet to be realized in practice.

The transformation of our mentality is accomplished through the procedure of conversion itself and not by comprehension. If it were the prerogative of the few with adequate acumen it would hardly advantage or apply to the whole of humanity. If the transformation of the human psyche from egocentrism to altruism required understanding it would benefit only the very select. But the criterion of the metamorphic reorientation of the soul is not privilege but openhearted sincerity.

Conceptual astuteness does not establish our essential reorientation because the intellect cannot demonstrate the conclusive existence of anything. Human reason calculates methodically alike to mathematics, gathering supportive or contradictory evidence but, through the oblique manner of its function, it is unable to arrive at definite knowledge except in terms of numerical computation.

Rationale is dependent upon the reliability of the particular evidence with which it is concerned because it cannot engage a situation directly and discover its intrinsic merit. As a function it serves the human being but it is not an entity itself and, consequently, it cannot immediately engage and directly experience a situation.

Merely understanding our human plight is insufficient and ineffective to its essential and urgent remediation, just as the will or imagination are inadequate through their inability to address the central issue of misidentification. They cannot change human orientation from the paucity of egocentrism to the plenitude of self-abnegation through supernal amity, because they are incommensurate faculties to the emphatic condition of being possessed by an entity. However, they may collectively steer us towards the appropriate remedy.

The peculiar predicament of self-misconception is the origin of all human confusion, meanness and abjection. It is exacerbated by our ignorance of the intrinsic distinction of other people as well as ourselves and through blindness to the essential significance of phenomena. Egocentrism is the restricted mentality of partiality and self-interest that essentially supersedes all other considerations. Yet through its segregation it is haunted by the suspicion of fundamental impermanence and insubstantiality because it resides in a state of innate isolation as if the separate self were solely significant although it knows that it is not.

We are prevented by self-circumscription from dimensional and qualitative expansion because we are disoriented through a perspective that is, first and foremost, endogenously established. While this is perfectly appropriate and prudent in disparate creatures who struggle for survival and the gratification of their instinctual drives, it is discreditable in the human being who has at once recognized a far more significant distinction than self-presumption.

Through coincidence within the accessible human heart, by proxy, we directly engage the fulfillment of our human destiny. We find that the antipodal sensibility to self-circumscription is an inclusive perspective established upon the way things exist in expansive reality. Thus, we recognize that our ignorance maintains a state of bondage that is only ameliorated through supernal intervention. The remoteness between self-preoccupation and the recognition of the intrinsic distinction of ourselves and every other person reveals just how faulty and unfounded our identification has become.

The intimate union through openhearted sincerity with the condition of our own human futurity permits us to embark upon the steadily increasing realization of our authentic existential status wherein we find that self-preoccupation is entirely absent. Remote, abstract segregation, that is the consequence of self-circumscription becomes an abhorrent condition, and we constantly seek instead to position ourselves within the expanse of The Immanent Presence. We find that our former egocentricity was entirely founded upon a deception that confined us to a merely superficial semblance of our authentic nature.

However, it should not for an instant be imagined that this reorientation of our singular, petty sense of identity towards the inclusive recognition of the essential distinction of ourselves and all other people, is accomplished through human will and effort. Should we suppose that we are able to encompass the spirit of Divine Love within our psyche through determination or personal virtue; we are merely indulging in wishful thinking and imaginative fiction. While resolute comity towards others would certainly benefit human affairs, the metamorphic translation of the human soul is not accomplished through personal resolution and aspiration.

It is a very good thing that we are unable to transform ourselves because human, self-circumscribed identification assumes many deceptive guises some of which even appear devout and saintly. But we do not want what we imagine our translated nature to be. We desire to become constant in constitution and demeanor with that which we experience of the Supernal Nature through openhearted susceptibility. Anything less derives from egocentrism because we cannot simply conjure up a new human paradigm of any significant meaningfulness. Fortunately, our translation is within far worthier hands than our own.

The Sistine Madonna by Italian painter Raphael (1483 - 1520)
The Madonna is portrayed absolutely without self-circumscription, qualitatively and essentially, entirely identified with the destiny of the Christ child and yet, simultaneously, a distinct individual.

20. Human Sovereign Autonomy

Through uncertainty concerning our existential status, destination and relevance, compounded by the inability to conclusively resolve the perplexity of our situation by reason or revelation, the human being can only hope to successfully manipulate circumstances towards personal advantage. We strive to make the best of a precarious and confusing predicament. This situation is exacerbated by religious and philosophical dogma and doctrine that is superficially established upon the merely physical appearance of things and, consequently, views circumstances from a materially defined and narrow viewpoint. Thus, so-called metaphysical reality, while conceptually intriguing, is little more that an extension of our existing corporeally circumscribed perspective. It may assuage our mystification through conviction but it neither acquaints nor guides us towards unequivocal certitude.

In order to establish the human psyche upon the freshness of unambiguous confidence, it is necessary to recognize that our conventional, cognitive transactions are inadequate to the task. Otherwise, we struggle continuously to achieve definitive intelligence concerning existence through inadequate means. Eventually, we merely compromise and select the approach that most closely accords with our own predilection or we fold to the prevailing consensus.

The manner whereby we restrain our habitual practices of cognition in order that we may immediately and experientially engage circumstances without distortion, require that we recognize our unique, singular distinction. It is the uniqueness of our intrinsic individuality that is our authentic particularity or human ipseity and not the body or its functions. Materialistic, Western philosophy insists that the corporeal contingency alone comprises the entirety of the human being. Upon the basis of this simplistic premise, further exploration and the discovery of the essential, human being is effectively arrested in the same manner whereby we remain ignorant of the intrinsic dimension of all phenomena through shallowness of vision.

The direct approach of the particular ipseity is possible because the human, singular distinction as an entity, is able to engage circumstances without intermediary interpretation. The intellectual approach is predictably indirect because as a corporeal faculty it is without identity and cannot experience. It calculates information and, through imagination establishes hypothetical possibilities but it is incapable of a direct encounter.

Similarly, knowledge acquired through intuitive discernment and feeling sentient evaluation, while evocative and intriguing, without the establishment of the human ipseity as the cognitive, sovereign principal, remains impossible to confirm. Perceptive sentiment is notoriously unreliable and frequently borders upon fantasy because not even the practitioner can be certain of its significance. If the oracles of Greek antiquity were enigmatic, in our modern times instinctual perceptivity is entirely unpredictable and as unproductive as speculation, it is more of a hindrance than a help.

Cognitive immediacy by the individual ipseity reveals both our own singular and unique distinction and that of others because we possess emphatic being and, consequently, we are able to encounter circumstances originally and instantaneously without the obstruction of translation and explication. But the human, self-circumscribed misidentification, through apprehensive autarchy, remains uncertain of its status and seeks to assert and advance its ambiguously established condition. Thus, it hinders the investiture of the singular distinction as the human, sovereign identity and cleaves to the superficial conceit of self-presumption.

      The remedy for the dilemma of egocentrism resides in a condition of immediacy within the contrite, human heart. Through direct cognition, the human ipseity discovers that the essential significance of all things exists immanently. Thus, supernal beneficence similarly establishes and occupies an immanent and intimate accord with the sincere and openhearted communicant and the essential reorientation of the human soul from self-centeredness to existential confidence is inaugurated. Through unequivocal amity, the pettiness of egocentrism is graciously superseded and we become steadily emancipated and advance towards our legitimate destiny of sovereign autonomy.

21. The Intrinsic Volume

It is clear that the manner of the essential reorientation of the human psyche from beleaguered self-circumscription towards the requisite and extraordinary recognition of human, intrinsic distinction, is beyond our capacity to hypothetically conceptualize. This is extremely fortuitous because otherwise we would endeavor to self-ameliorate our condition with predictably lamentable consequences. We cannot reestablish ourselves upon a rehabilitated, existential foundation unless it is already in our possession and if that were the case, remediation would be unnecessary. All that is required of us is the earnest desire and readiness to permit The Immanent Presence access to our innermost psychology. Subsequently, our future condition becomes effectively beyond our egocentric concern because we are without the means to secure or to establish the nature of the new paradigm. Thus, we do not achieve the metamorphic reestablishment of the human psyche through our own competence; it is given to us through grace.

Openhearted sincerity describes the necessary approach towards emancipation while opening the heart to The Immanent Presence characterizes the means whereby the expansive perspective supersedes insular self-circumscription. The reorientation of the human psyche establishes a contradictory ethos within the heart whereupon our entire perspective moves away from concern with the petty sense-of-self and we thereby discover the full volume of existence which is reality.

It is unimaginable for the myopic, self-preoccupied

mentality to comprehend its own essential misrepresentation but nonetheless through self-circumscription we misconstrue our identity and assume existential conditions that are obsolete and without prospect. We are ignorant of our authentic distinction, and we adopt a counterfeit status. Oblivious to the reality, we engage circumstances superficially mistaking the corporeal appearance of ourselves and others as the entirety while we suppose that the physical conditions of phenomena comprise the composite.

Through the contrition of a healthy conscience coupled with essential disquietude, the heart becomes vulnerable to the transformative impact that an immediate experience of the full volume of reality has upon it. Self-absorption is succeeded by an omniscient compass that reveals the actual status of existence whereby the intrinsic meaningfulness of things becomes unequivocal.

It is clearly evident that egocentrism is obstructive to immediate cognition because the preoccupation of self-interest establishes a merely subjective acquaintance towards circumstances. The viewpoint of the self-circumscribed mentality is inevitably limited because it is fundamentally established upon the pettiness of the overestimation of oneself as exclusively preeminent.

Self-interest presents only very conditional prospects for human advancement because it is a status that is at variance with essential reality. The human, authentic identification recognizes the intrinsic certainty of its existence and does not require emotional augmentation. From the viewpoint of the human ipseity, the immediate experience of personal uniqueness is qualified by the recognition of the singular distinction of others and thereby to do them harm amounts to self-infliction.

Through immediate cognition, we authenticate the existence of the meaningful volume of existence. The human ipseity recognizes the similarly unique distinction of others, and it is not threatened thereby because it finds its own intrinsic significance to be inviolate and beyond challenge. The conviction of exclusive, personal relevance rests upon the erroneous assumption of particular and segregated importance. This essential and entrenched misconception is beyond the reach of human competence and genius to remedy but requires supernal intervention.

The rueful heart turns towards The Immanent Presence and subsequently finds that self-circumscription is suspended, and we engage the reality of an expansive and inclusive existence that is undistorted by self-overestimation. Through intimate and candid concurrence with The Immanent Presence, we recognize that the manner whereby we approach the intrinsic consequence of others is the same as that by which we ourselves are essentially known.

22. The Constant Presence

The urgency of our time is to address the essential malaise that hinders human progress and obscures the imperative objective of requisite maturation. The dynamic whereby the obsolete mentality of self-circumscription is transmuted through constitutive reorientation can no longer be concealed by human misrepresentation but must become blatantly obvious in its essential simplicity without distortion.

We no longer possess the leisure to allow ourselves to be captivated by a tiresome reiteration of clichéd, exhausted doctrine that promises reward and endowment that no human agency is empowered to dispense. Nor is it prudent to concur with the assertions of an arrogant, scientific elite that are constrained within the selective parameters of exclusive materialism. They disdain the volume and meaningful proportions of existence upon the naive presumption of physically absolute circumstances that cannot independently exist. Materialistic, Western philosophy is established upon the abstract conviction of the exclusionary significance of the form and structure of phenomena without qualitative extension, which presents an affected imitation deprived of intrinsic importance.

The evasion of the essential necessity of human, dispositional transformation is prolonged at our peril because we face a steady regression of the human ethos as a consequence of our neglect. The indulgence of self-antecedence intensifies segregation and disassociation from the authentic conditions of existence because it assumes a fractious, essential rivalry that is a counterfeit, human individualism.

The central issue facing humanity is a distorted perspective towards existence that originates with an essentially erroneous conviction of preeminent self-importance, further compounded by materialistic myopia. Self-circumscription has no future not only because it essentially contradicts reality but by virtue of the mayhem that inevitably ensues from uninhibited avarice. Ignorance of the authentic condition and status of the human, cardinal constitution inevitably demeans humanity and reduces a tenuous ethnology to a combative and antagonistic battle for self-interest.

The complacent and privileged few disregard the decline of global culture because the urgency does not appear to encroach too severely upon their amenity. They assume a position of cavalier disdain towards matters of essential divinity and morality as if dismissal provided them with an alternative to reality. But when we cast our gaze upon the general plight of humanity, the consequences of self-absorption and ignorance are overtly conspicuous and their traditional remediation appears chimerical.

Therefore, we abandon the facade of self-preeminence and the apparent security and indifference offered by material prosperity in order to approach existence from the perspective of unambiguous impartiality. From a forthright and openhearted aspect, we recognize that our superficial perspective has little significant merit, and we embark upon an exploration of the profound. Eventually, as with all sincere and honest endeavor, the expedient approach becomes evident and we find ourselves encountering two convergent imperatives. Through direct cognition we inevitably discover our own essential distinction and we determine that it is entirely without self-predominance. It exists within an immediate association to the intrinsic status of all other things.

Thus, an entire dimension and relevance to existence become evident, and we yearn to promote its investiture within our sensibility as an invariable significance. However, we find ourselves hampered by a moribund yet habituated predisposition that prevents its consistent realization and seeks to preserve existing conditions.

In view of the impasse before us and in recognition of the futility of self-amelioration, the sincere investigator soon discovers the existence of an immanent, antecedent corrective. Through openhearted sincerity, the reconstruction of the human psyche upon the foundation of essential realism is inaugurated and we recommence our journey towards our destined maturity established upon amity and goodwill. We welcome a morality that is founded upon deference for the unique, intrinsic singularity of others and through our own direct experience of the essential significance of things, we encounter the full consequence of existence.

23. One Reality

Through the restraint of conventional perception which consists primarily of the interpretative faculties of the intellect and feeling-sentience, we establish the crucial conditions imperative to immediate cognition. The human, authentic identification and unique distinction is congruently established with the essential of all phenomena through immanent and contiguous relationship. This condition is directly engaged through the straightforward, experiential percipience of the human ipseity. Nothing stands between the authentic and uniquely singular distinction of the individual and its recognition of intrinsic existence. Thus, the nature of the elemental status of inanimate phenomena; the conceptual inception of all organic life and its particular, qualitative expression, and human, intrinsic singularity become unambiguously evident.

The direct occupation of a situation from the viewpoint of the human ipseity facilitates the activity of essential cognition. The state of deliberately established immediacy brings intrinsic circumstances to our attention, and we discover the full dimension of their existence beyond the merely physical appearance. Oblique, conventional perception, absorbed with only superficial information concerning phenomena, obscures the essential condition. Through our familiar manner of perception, we are unable to conclusively accomplish definitive identification because intrinsic circumstances are only determined by the direct, experiential engagement of the human entity itself. Therefore, conventionally, we can only perceive things for their general and inconsiderable palpability while the intangible volume remains obscured from our corporeal faculties of awareness.

Corporeal established, cognitive faculties cannot experience, but they assess and interpret information based upon prior acumen or preferential bias. However, the essential person is not a function but an intrinsic identity which is alone capable of immediate cognition because its approach is unalloyed by intermediary interpretation.

Thus, the full spectrum of existence is discovered through the direct engagement of circumstances and therein we confirm the authenticity of The Immanent Presence. That which we discover through openhearted sincerity is corroborated through the immediate encounter of the emergent, human ipseity. We find ourselves delighted but not astonished because there is no other existence except reality and therein we would expect The Immanent Presence to reside.

This discovery greatly expedites the conversion of self-circumscription towards the establishment of the ipseity as the human, sovereign distinction because we find The Immanent Presence readily accessible and we do not have to rely upon hope and faith. The reality of supernal amity and goodwill is settled beyond doubt. Thereby we recognize the sublime antithesis of egocentricity through personal encounter and the inevitable reorientation of our obsolete self is assured.

It becomes almost unbearable not to be within The Immanent Presence because otherwise we endure a dearth of quality and significance in a condition that resembles an unpleasant fiction remote from reality. Our own meager resources and the endless privation of a false sense of identity, compared with the intimate concurrence with The Immanent Presence, seems an affective wasteland.

Above all things we desire to maintain our intimacy with supernal beneficence because, increasingly, we become disdainful of our former condition. We aspire to enter immediately into this intimate concurrence as our primary aspiration which of itself emboldens our determination. From the perspective of openhearted sincerity, we find that we discover things directly as they exist in their fullness, not as the result of some obscure mystical experience but through constant eagerness. Thereby we resolve both the materialistic myopia that preoccupies human kind and the dilemma of our own self-circumscription and its subsequent aberrations.

Without the constancy of The Presence we are easily deceived by the duplicity of myriad counterfeit attestations purporting to explain existence, but which merely arise from uncertain imagination and the desire of self-importance. The gauge of authenticity that decides whether or not we legitimately maintain communion with The Immanent Presence and do not merely deceive ourselves or allow ourselves to be deceived, rests upon the manner whereby we regard phenomena. If our engagement with circumstances is merely superficial, then we cannot claim to be resident within the circumference of The Immanent Presence. Nothing is superficial to openhearted sincerity, but we inevitably ascertain the fullness of phenomenal existence.

The rift between conventional perception and

immediate engagement is an easily recognizable qualitative discrepancy. The distilled, physical properties that we typically assume to comprise the full extent of reality are discovered to be superficial from the moment that we enter The Immediate Presence. We find that the qualitative volume is unrelated to physical proportion and that essential distinction is physically elusive but intrinsically evident. We become alert to the full substance of things through the same manner whereby we find them by immediate engagement. Everything is distinguished for its essential significance and similarly we recognize the intrinsic singularity that differentiates one person from another and exists independently of the physical appearance.

24. Corporeal Myopia

We do not require imagination in order to discover the intrinsic nature of things. In fact, ingenuity is entirely converse to direct cognition. Our purpose is not to comprehend the intrinsic distinction that epitomizes, for example, a native-element-mineral nor to envisage the qualitative particularity of an individual color. The immediate approach is not dependent upon forethought or realization but requires the repositioning of our perspective away from the corporeal intellect and the establishment of the non-physical, human ipseity as our viewpoint.

Existence is not a problem in need of a solution nor a riddle that requires an answer. In order to discover the elemental condition of things, we cannot apply conceptualization because intellection is only appropriate to the resolution of a quandary. It is meaningless in terms of identification because it is of incommensurate relevance to the task. Therefore, our human challenge lies in the manner of our conventional perception towards existence which is wholly inadequate to the discovery of the essential status of things.

The imaginative conceptualization of probable explanation will always fail us when applied to essential existence. The definitive identification of circumstances and the discovery of the intrinsic significance of things is unacknowledged through conjecture. In order to conclusively distinguish the inherent particularity of something, the intellectually imperceptible volume of the phenomenon must be recognized. This is unachievable through astuteness and predetermination but requires direct confrontation through the human ipseity in order to attain definitive identification.

Through immediate cognition, we discover the conceptual architecture and qualitative caliber of physical composition, as the overlooked volume of its existence. We do not reason or deduce the existence of the elusive origin of resolute arrangement in the manner of the intellectual, nor entangle ourselves in the compelling ramifications of a hypothesis. These preoccupations merely divert us from the direct, experiential approach and limit the possibility of original knowledge. If we wish to discover the essential condition of circumstances, it is crucial to avoid abstract evaluation. If we assume that we can weigh and appraise and thereby determine the intrinsic nature of existence, we deceive ourselves and detract from the discovery of the actual circumstances.

The full dimension of the existence of a phenomenon cannot be assessed through rationalization because the activity of deliberation is an oblique and indirect function. Deduction deflects our attention away from the possibility of the direct encounter, wherein the inherent status of something is spontaneously discovered, and towards the uncertain realm of oblique estimation.

The intellectual practices of analytical deduction are appropriate to the discovery of the workings of things. But the manner of function answers the question *how* and not *what* something is. If we try to apply the means whereby, we ascertain the mechanisms of things to the discovery of their identity we merely corrupt our inquiry through an unsuitable cognitive strategy that is inappropriate to the task. Thereby the identity of something becomes established upon its activity or physical properties, and we occupy ourselves with the imponderable mystery of the reason why something functions as if its significance resided solely within the mechanism.

The pertinent investigation of existence commences with the identification of circumstances that is not established upon the sum of the physical functions but the intrinsic significance of the entirety. Through immediate cognition, we confront a phenomenon and discover the elemental status of its existence. Thereby we find the answer to the question *why* because it coincides inherently with the particular distinction.

It is upon the basis of cognitive misapplication that we have developed a conceptual facsimile of existence, that is entirely composed of contrivances and physical structure. Existence itself has become interpreted from the particular perspective of general physics, and we consequently find ourselves with an entirely, physically exclusive explanation of life that is severely to our detriment. Not only is the solely material perspective superficial, the conviction of an exclusionary physicality segregates us from the meaningful volume of existence wherein all relevance and value resides. Thus, we occupy a humanly fabricated perception of life that pollutes even the boldest theology because we argue on behalf of spirituality in physical terms whereby it is incomprehensibly re-rendered through the perspective of exclusive materiality.

Entrenched materialistic, Western philosophy is not the privileged domain of the intellectual. It permeates our entire ethos. It is the customary, cognitive approach even when we discuss incorporeal existence. It is through a pervasive preoccupation with the blatant physical condition of things that we endeavor to interpret life solely in those terms and thereby the suggestion of intangible volume conjures up the fictional imagery of rarefied physical conditions or alternative universes. The existence of an immanently extant, incorporeal dimension that belies physical exclusivity and lends everything significance and meaningfulness, or of the emphatic statement of human, incorporeal continuity, is seen as an inconceivable excess.

      Thus, we hinder our own further development towards cognitive and existential liberty through a shortsighted fixation with the appearances of things Through our material preoccupation we fail to recognize essential significance. All the while the remedy for this predicament is already positioned for our emancipation. But we imagine that we precociously comprehend existence from our exclusively material point-of-view and thereby we confound our own extrication through counter-productive pretension.

25. The Twin Restrictions

Two implicit obstacles within the human psyche impede individual emancipation towards a liberty of a sovereign autonomy that is established upon our essential, incorporeal distinction. Increasingly, popular ideology suggests that existential liberation is synonymous with self-indulgence and personal gratification. Therefore, every means is pursued towards its attainment with disastrous social consequences wherein the aspirations and inclinations of each may take precedent over the civic well-being of the majority. The counterfeit of liberation is unrestrained license which only exacerbates human, materialistic subjugation.

The parallel impediments to human emancipation are egocentrism and a materialistic, Western philosophy which presumes that significance resides with the exclusively physical condition of things. The one gives confidence to the stance of the other and consolidates human obliviousness to the meaningful extent of existence.

Self-circumscription is a humanly insurmountable obstacle because the conviction of individual exception is thoroughly entrenched within the psyche. Self-preeminence necessarily obscures the reality of the mutual, individual significance of everyone else. In desperate circumstances the human race relinquishes all cultural and social cohesion and devolves into rancor for personal advantage. We endeavor only selectively to renounce egotism when it is expedient to do so through service to a higher consideration than our own preference. But if abnegation is personally expedient, it becomes itself, egocentrically driven. Thus, the abstemious and devoted mystic may be blissfully indifferent to the plight of everyone else.

The twin restrictions towards human emancipation and authentic liberation are overwhelming because of our misidentification with a petty sense of the mortal selfhood. However, the human, intrinsic identity is entirely, existentially confident and of a magnanimous caliber that is unequivocally established upon personal continuance. The human, incorporeally extant ipseity is imperturbably selfless because its existence is emphatically assured. Thus, unlike the petty sense-of-self, it requires neither aggrandizement nor defense.

The way forward is one that is far easier than we could ever imagine because our reorientation of identity away from self-circumscription towards altruism does not require human accomplishment. But through traditional misrepresentation, the essential condition of immanent, non-physical existence and the ready ministrations of supernal beneficence have been obscured until to the candid observer even the transparent objective of human, dispositional metamorphosis appears to be a fictional chicanery.

Contaminated by artifice and ignorance, the straightforward approach of discrete and respective openhearted sincerity towards The Immanent Presence has accumulated asinine overtones of superstition and magic. Wary of the deception, the pragmatist rejects the esoteric approach and endeavors to postulate concerning existence solely through the assimilation of materially substantial evidence. Of itself, this is not an entirely futile approach because the discovery of the immanent volume of existence is quite definitely feasible through impartial empiricism from the viewpoint of the human, essential identity.

The solution to the human predicament of existential uncertainty, lies within the fabric of existence itself and not in some contrived structure of our own manufacture. We fail to recognize the essential status and condition of things because we do not engage circumstances directly. The immediate encounter requires the viewpoint of the human ipseity and remains unattainable through conventional, associative cognition.

Through the recognition and the establishment of the human, intrinsic distinction as the dominant perspective towards phenomena, we discover the overlooked essential volume of material existence without which there exists neither meaningfulness nor purpose. Thus, impartial empiricism through the viewpoint of the human ipseity reveals the authentic structure of existence while openhearted sincerity towards The Immanent Presence steadily establishes the crucial, exemplary stature that is essential to human maturation.

26. Catharsis

We enter into an intimate concurrence with The Immanent Presence through openhearted sincerity and thereby we discover and directly engage a supernal virtue that entirely without egotism. We experience the nature of righteousness combined with an unequivocal amity and concord towards us. With increasing familiarity, we resolve to abandon our instinctive apprehension and the traditional concepts of a punitive Deity because the heart assures us of the benignity of immanent goodwill and we have no need of defensiveness.

However, we find ourselves inhibited by a qualitative discrepancy. We find our human, idiosyncratic complexion at odds with the benevolence and generosity that we now confront. The disparity is starkly revealed, and we find ourselves wanting. The purgative catharsis that ensues is entirely of our own initiation. We desire to admonish and expunge ourselves of our obsolete disposition because the kindness that we experience essentially within our susceptible heart motivates our earnestness.

An analogous parallel of Natural metamorphosis readily comes to mind as we renounce our former and now redundant condition in the expectancy of a new and unknown status but one that we are certain is akin to our direct experience of The Immanent Presence.

Thus, we recognize that there is no supernal retribution but merely the necessity of reorientation. The pandemonium that ensues from unrestrained egotism and correlative materialism is misery enough as a cursory contemplation of the human, global plight clearly corroborates. A deity would have no interest in our prolonged ordeal and would merely wishes to transpose our anachronistic mentality in order that we may enjoy the fullness of reality.

Our disappointing, inadequate disposition is steadily ameliorated through contrition because we find ourselves qualitatively juxtaposed against the embodiment of our own destined condition. We confirm and authenticate that this is the case because we have already glimpsed the nature of reality through immediate cognition and we have discovered the human ipseity. There is no other legitimate status except reality. Anything else is the misleading result of a moribund and constricted mentality which limits us to a mere aspect of existence that in its isolation presents the illusion of the entirety.

But a constitutional transformation is not ours to perform. Our self-circumscribed mentality prevents us from its accomplishment. Our task is to thoroughly embrace the process and willingly welcome its attainment but not to attempt our own metamorphosis. It is the sincerity of our approach that initiates the essential communion with The Immanent Presence while the locus of our reformation lies within the accessible, human heart.

The intellect, established upon the conviction of an exclusively corporeal existence, will have none of this and will deride it as delusional. But we have approached the issue of the necessary reestablishment of the human psyche with meticulous care and discovered the authenticity of supernal intervention. Furthermore, we find that there is no other effective approach because all else relies upon an essentially dysfunctional egocentricity that is incapable of performing the necessary transition because within its own maladjustment lies the dilemma.

We should be overjoyed that the prospect of human, essential transformation does not require our expertise and that we can submit our sad disposition to The Immanent Presence and permit the consummation of our own metamorphosis. Through immediate cognition we are fully alert to the overlooked volume of existence that lies beyond conventional perception and we welcome our prospective admission.

27. Misperception

If we imagine that human transformation occurs somehow magically while we continue to indulge aspects of a fictional interpretation of existence, we fail to grasp the distinction between reverie and reality. The expectation of some other context or occasion wherein we suddenly discover the authentic nature of things, obscure the necessity of the transformation of our perspective and imply that the modification of our self-circumscribed temperament occurs independently of our mentality.

While reality is certainly obscured by the superficial manner of human perception, obliviousness does not signify that certainty occupies a different place or condition. Reality is always conspicuous as the authentic state of existence when we encounter circumstances immanently. Reality is necessarily engaged immediately and not in some alternative landscape of our own conception.

We cannot advance cognitively while we maintain a distorted viewpoint because thereby we merely compound our ignorance and assume that reality resides as a dimension of a humanly confused fabrication. The old mentality and manner of perception wherein we egocentrically position ourselves towards circumstances must be entirely superseded because it is obstructive to immediate engagement and continues to conceal reality. Misperception is at fault otherwise we would readily engage the fullness of existence which is, of course, an extant but unrealized condition and not a different place.

The dimensional expansion of human

discernment must be wholeheartedly undertaken. We cannot simultaneously indulge both ignorance and merely upon a whim enter the direct experience of the authentic state of existence because the two are entirely incommensurate conditions. There is only one reality. Everything else rests upon an erroneous point-of-view that perceives things superficially and subjectively. Whatever we assume, concerning existence does not influence the way things really are, one iota. It merely alters our experience.

The conditions inspired by a superficial perspective or one that is abstractly fabricated, cannot be converted into reality by any agency be it almighty or humanly wishful. Falsehood establishes an illusory situation that in the light of the immediate experience of reality is recognized as non-existent. Therefore, that which appears as a consequence of misperception only really exists as an extension of a shallow and ignorant point-of-view.

We will always remain dissatisfied with an imperfect representation of existence because the conventional, cognitive approaches of oblique perception, abstract conceptualization and subjective sentience do not address circumstances directly but present only an inferred counterpart. If we approach existence circumstantially and attempt to discover volume in the apparent, we merely compound conjecture with further assumed knowledge. Without intangible dimension, existence becomes meaningless to us.

Immediate, experiential cognition alone reveals the authentic circumstances of things. We cannot sustain a preference for some aspects of our misconception, but everything must be immanently engaged in order that we may discover reality. Otherwise, we contradict our own direct experience of existence through ambivalence. A mere suggestion of reality does not dispel human benightedness, but straightforward engagement without partiality is required in order that we may identify the intrinsic significance of existence.

28. Immanence

Through the immediate, cognitive engagement of circumstances, we enter into a relationship of immanence wherein we discover the intrinsic and meaningful volume of things. This elemental condition is also where we encounter the essential distinction of ourselves and other people. Thus, we identify the full estate of existence of which the physical context is determined to be the consummation of intangible conditions that are commonly encountered only in the most peripheral manner.

Immediate engagement is accomplished through the restraint of conventional perception and the establishment of the human ipseity as the seat of cognition. Thus, through our own essential distinction, we are able to directly discover the essential status of everything else without the intermediary translation of reason or through affective evaluation. Essential circumstances are found to exist in a condition that is elusive to our corporeal, cognitive faculties and incomprehensible to the mentality that considers that the entirety of existence is exclusively physically represented.

The elemental condition of things exists emphatically without spatial coordinates or subjugation to time. But it is not an alternative realm. It is the neglected volume of meaningfulness that is absent from the philosophy of physical exclusivity that merely portrays the structural attributes as if they were the entirety of phenomena. It is within this explicit, intangible volume that all intrinsic significance resides as the particular distinction and qualitative dimension of phenomena, and the conceptual objective of organic architecture.

The physical belies the intrinsic dimension of the existence of things that are readily overlooked because we have become accustomed to exclusively material pertinence. While the qualitative value of things is recognized through subjective experience, we only confidently ascribe significance to those properties that can be quantified because thereby their existence is established beyond doubt. But search as we may, the intrinsic meaningfulness of existence can never be found through a physical scrutiny of material conditions because it is only implied by the appearances of things and otherwise it remains elusive.

From the perspective of the singular and uniquely distinct, human identification, we are able to ascertain the full volume of existence because human ipseity exists immanently and emphatically without corporeal necessity. Thus, the essential condition of human singularity, because of its elemental significance, is able to determine through the certainty of its own original existence, the authenticity of every philosophical, metaphysical or abstract contention.

The crux of the immediate engagement of circumstances in order to ascertain the full volume of their existence, is the recognition of the human, unique and sovereign distinction. The ipseity discovers its own significance and upon that basis it is able to navigate successfully through all presumptive doctrine and philosophy. It is not deceived by analytical deliberation or persuasive polemic nor by metaphysical conviction because its own existence endures emphatically as an ultimate reality.

Two extremes of perception reside within the

human psyche. The one is established upon a conviction of the exclusive physicality of existence while the other is founded upon an abstract rationale conjured without empirical context. They exist in uneasy tension and can only be successfully resolved through the intercession of the human ipseity. The ipseity regards materialistic, Western philosophy and finds it superficial, a perspective void of meaning and volume. Similarly, the singular, intrinsic distinction which is the authentic human identification that resides in a condition of incorporeal immanence, examines abstract conceptualization and finds it wanting. The cogency of both deductive rational and theoretical conviction does not persuade nor impress the viewpoint of imperative existence.

The one certainty and the only absolute within the immediate reach of human discernment remains the infallibility of our own intrinsic existence. The ipseity regards circumstances from the authority of its own existential assurance whereby everything may be tried for its tenor be it metaphysical conviction, philosophical abstraction or the exclusivity of materialism. All these contentions and assertions may be qualitatively weighed for their authenticity against the certainty of the individual, intrinsic significance.

Furthermore, from the perspective of the human ipseity, through immediate cognition, we discover in the overlooked meaningfulness and volume of existence, that which corroborates our own existential certainty. We recognize the essential distinction of others and of all phenomena.

However, human kind suffers from a benighted morality established upon a self-circumscribed disposition that hinders the development of sovereign autonomy. The petty sense-of-self is convinced of a personal precedence, a position that is only subdued through cultural restraint from becoming rampant. But established within the condition of immanent existence resides a remedial countermeasure that ameliorates egocentrism and concomitant malice and assures human maturation.

      Our essential task is to accommodate our dispositional transformation through openhearted sincerity and vulnerability towards The Presence of Amity. Our obsolete self is transformed through reorientation not by human effort but by the goodness and grace of supernal intervention. But we do not have to merely believe because through immediate cognition we discover the inherent volume of existence wherein we find there also resides human emancipation.

Other Books by the Same Author

TOWARDS A MEANINGFUL FUTURE
The Continuum of the Qualitative Expansion of the Soul

THE IMMANENT PRINCIPLE OF INTEGRITY AND GOODWILL
The Integration of the Principle of Virtue within the Human heart

THE EVOLUTIONARY IMPERATIVE OF OUR TIME
The Crucial Establishment of an Inspired Ethos with the Individual, Human Heart, appropriate to a Meaningful Future

RECONCILIATION WITH HUMAN DESTINY
The Surrender of the Heart-of-the-Soul as the Expedient Approach Towards Direct Engagement with the Immanent Exemplar of a Future, Human Disposition

THE QUALITATIVE EVOLUTION OF THE SOUL
The Evolutionary Transformation of the Human Soul Through Openhearted Sincerity Towards Immanent Caritas

THE SUPERNAL ETHOS
Unanimity with the Divine Nature

THE BEGINNING OF WISDOM
Knowledge through Immediate Engagement

UNDER THE AEGIS OF IMMANENT CARITAS
The Reorientation of the Human, Disparate Self-circumscribed Mentality

THE DECEPTION OF MATERIALISTIC WESTERN PHILOSOPHY
An Exploration of the Physically Elusive Volume of Existence

THE MEANINGFUL VOLUME OF EXISTENCE
An Exploration of the Overlooked Intangible Significance of Phenomena

HUMAN SOVEREIGN AUTONOMY
The Discovery of the Human Ipseity and its Establishment as the Essential Authority of the Human Constitution

THE TRANSFORMATION OF THE SOUL
From Self-centeredness to Sovereign Autonomy

THE IMPLICATION OF HUMAN, INCORPOREAL EXISTENCE
The Overlooked Significance of the Intangible and Qualitative Dimension of Existence

IMMEDIATE EXPERIENTIAL COGNITION
The Inherent Human Capacity of Immediate Engagement

KNOWLEDGE THROUGH DIRECT COGNITION
The Human Conscious Individuality and Immediately Experienced Reality

www.ingramcontent.com/pod-product-compliance
Lightning Source LLC
Chambersburg PA
CBHW070814100426
42742CB00012B/2355